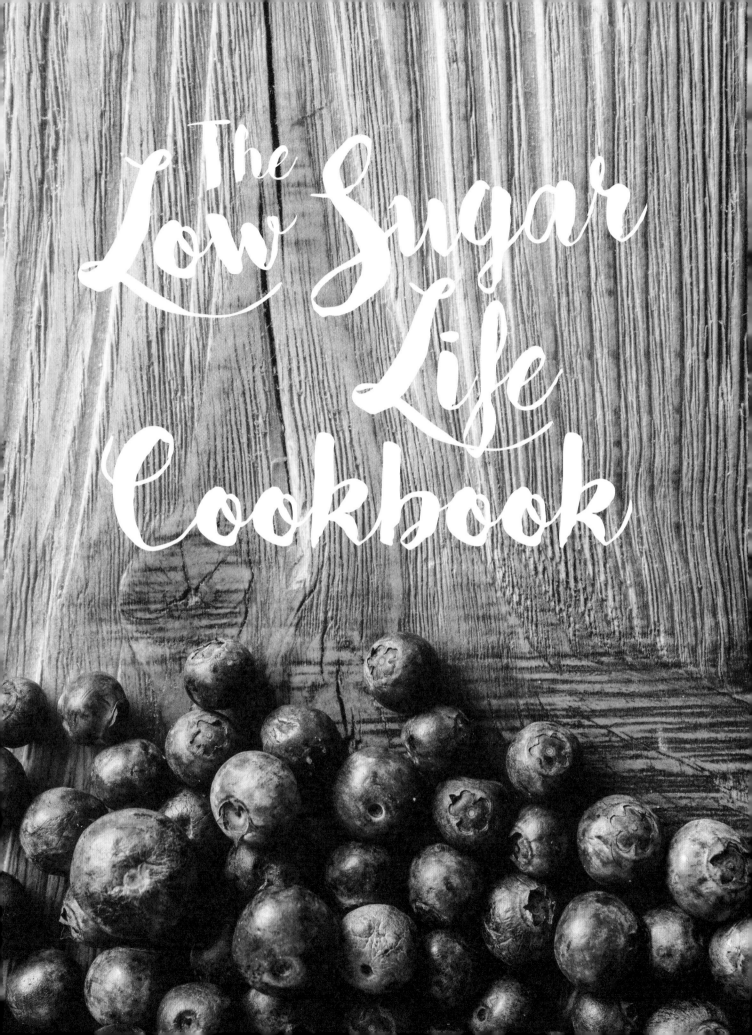

The Low Sugar Life Cookbook

CONTENTS

INTRODUCTION

Low sugar! No sugar! It's a catch-cry of the moment in health-food circles. But why should you care? Easy answer: spikes in blood sugar can cause mood swings and weight gain. Grr. But, also, the liver is the only organ in the body able to break down the fructose found in processed sugar, and it is thought that the poor liver can't cope with the sugar we are sending its way. Impaired liver function has been linked to chronic diseases such as diabetes, heart disease, obesity and cancer, so it's a good idea to be nice to your liver.

Okay, now what? It's processed sugar that we are really trying to avoid, because it contains high levels of fructose. This simple fact opens the door to a vast world of potential (and confusion), because there are so many other ways to get your sugar fix than just from processed white sugar. That's where this book comes in. We'll make it simple for you: we outline the basic principles of low sugar eating, highlight the important ingredients (what to embrace and what to avoid) and present easy recipes for you to enjoy. The approach we take in this book is one of moderation: eliminate a few things, embrace many things, and indulge occasionally.

Breakfast provides a great opportunity to start the day as you mean to go on. In a low sugar world, breakfast could mean protein — protein is important in low sugar diets because of the role it plays in reducing sugar cravings — and that may mean eggs. We offer some great ways to get egged up in the morning, from 'green scrambled' to a beautiful but simple omelette, or kick-start the day with fiery home-fried eggs with chilli sauce. A smoothie bowl is a fun way to enjoy breakfast and stock up on the good stuff. Try the super-berry acai for a rich red breakfast bowl that's high on antioxidants and will aid digestion and circulation. Or, if you fancy something sweet for breakfast, why not try the matcha green tea brownies or dark chocolate quinoa bowl?

In the lunch section of this book, you'll find hot tips for making your favourite foods in low sugar form. How about burgers, but without the traditional white bun? White bread, along with white pasta and rice, is something we recommend in moderation, and if you can develop a taste for the brown versions then that's all to your benefit. Brown rice and whole-wheat bread and pasta contain higher levels of fibre and help stabilize blood sugar levels. Bread aside, imagine sweet potato, eggplant or portobello mushroom as a substitute for a burger bun. It's such a cool idea that looks and tastes great. Another tip: use cauliflower fritters as the bread in your sandwich — a quirky idea that delivers more fun, flavour and nutrients than the traditional bread sandwich.

Family dinners can continue to be whatever you are used to but with a low sugar twist, whether that be a simple risotto (try it with brown rice), moussaka, meatballs, fish or the classic roast dinner. Try the variation on a roast chicken in this section of the book, which has an amazing chickpea stuffing for extra oomph. Also in this section, discover barley and why it might make an interesting choice for your family's dinnertime.

In the snacks section, we offer plenty of savoury and sweet options. For savoury, try kale chips or embrace wonder-vegetable spinach recreated in tarts, muffins or pancakes. For the sweet stuff, try exploring alternatives to

Low

[low] **adjective**

of lesser degree, size, or amount
than average or ordinary

— MERRIAM-WEBSTER

plain white flour. We give an overview of the why and the what, and provide recipes that allow you to test out different flours in cookies, cakes and slices.

Desserts are the stomping ground of low sugar advocates and many a classic has been recreated. We have some great recipes here for new takes on old favourites, such as raw cashew cheesecake or black bean brownies. These clever tricks add nutrients at the same time as they reduce fructose, so it's a win-win. Also in this section, you'll find plenty of indulgent treats that may be low on sugar but don't shy away from fat. We explore why full fat is a good thing and celebrate cream in all its deliciousness. You can't have cream without vanilla bean and you'll also discover the low-down here on the various forms that vanilla takes. Those serious about reducing their fructose intake will come to know and love certain fruits more than others due to the natural fructose content, which can vary greatly from a melon to a blackberry, for example. Berries are generally a friend of low sugar diets, and we celebrate them here as the star ingredient of cake, parfait, mousse, soufflé and tart.

Low sugar doesn't have to be a po-faced affair: you can party like the best of them. In this section, we offer ideas for healthy versions of classic party foods from finger-licking drumsticks, kebabs and fishcakes to salads and sausage rolls. Also here you will find ideas for dinner-party food from scallops to chocolate pudding. You'll be amazed at what you can achieve, and your friends will be too.

Enjoy *The Low Sugar Life!*

Breakfast

SMOOTHIE BOWLS

Smoothie bowls are all the rage. Instead of blending fruit, yoghurt and granola and drinking the mixture through a straw, the ingredients are presented in a bowl. They're jam-packed with more fibre and vitamins than the classic bowl of cereal with milk, plus they're more fun to eat than a smoothie. Every spoonful of a smoothie bowl can be different.

From above, they look like nothing but goodness: oats or granola, layered with bright purees, with gorgeous fruits, nuts and interesting seeds scattered all about. There is a tricky reality, however: these can be high in calories and also bursting with sugar. Some restaurants and juice bars use fruit sorbets or fruit juice, often packed with added sugar. They might also use flavoured yoghurts and sweetened nuts, or fruit that has been stewed, or sweeteners like maple syrup that are fine in moderation but, if overdone, may lead to a blood sugar spike.

TIPS FOR SELF-CONTROL

Skip the honey or ask for raw honey, which has nutrients and medicinal qualities.

Ask for fresh fruit, plain yoghurt and ice or coconut water instead of sorbet.

Granola is typically high-calorie — opt for raw oats or muesli, or skip it and focus on fruits and seeds.

Consider eating just half the smoothie bowl, and pay attention to when the belly is full. Exercising portion control is an excellent way to start forming new habits.

GOOD SMOOTHIE BOWL TOPPINGS

BLUEBERRIES: Berries have lower fructose levels and higher fibre than most fruits, so are a good option to add natural sweetness. They also come packed with vitamin C and antioxidants.

FLAXSEEDS: The oil in flaxseeds is packed with healthy omega-3 fats and fibre, which is key to balancing blood sugar levels after eating. This balance is essential in the prevention of type 2 diabetes and heart disease. Two tablespoons of the seeds or the oil in a smoothie should do the trick.

HEMPSEEDS: Fluffy and cream-coloured when removed from the hull, hempseeds are rich in fibre, gluten-free, and bursting with nutrients including good omega-3 and omega-6 fats.

COCONUT: The white flesh of this tropical fruit is full of fibre that is essential for digestion and absorption of vitamins. Sprinkle on organic flakes for a buttery crunch and also for iron, vitamin C and a handful of the crucial vitamin Bs.

Matcha Smoothie Bowl

SERVES 2

2 cups (400g, 14oz) fresh pineapple, chopped

2 bananas, peeled

1 small bunch spinach, washed

2 kiwi fruits, peeled

½ ripe avocado, peeled and pitted

1 tsp culinary grade matcha powder

TOPPINGS

½ cup (50g, 2oz) blueberries, rinsed

1 kiwi fruit, peeled and sliced

⅓ cup (40g, 1½ oz) walnuts, toasted and chopped

¼ cup (20g, ¾ oz) sliced coconut

2 tsps chia seeds

1 tsp flaxseeds

1 tbsp pepitas (pumpkin seeds)

½ lime, thinly sliced

1 tsp bee pollen

Place ingredients for the smoothie into a blender and process until smooth. Pour the smoothie into two bowls and finish with the suggested toppings, or toppings of your choice.

Melon & Mango Refresher

SERVES 2

2 kiwi fruits, peeled and sliced

½ cantaloupe, peeled and cubed

1 whole mango, peeled, pitted and cubed

½ cup (125ml, 4fl oz) coconut water

1 small banana

TOPPINGS

1 kiwi fruit, sliced

2 tbsps goji berries

¼ cup (20g, ¾ oz) desiccated coconut

2 tbsps chia seeds

Place ingredients for the smoothie into a blender and process until smooth.

Pour the smoothie into two bowls and finish with the suggested toppings, or toppings of your choice.

BEE POLLEN

How about this: skip the honey and instead, take some bee pollen in your smoothie or over your cereal. Pollen is a byproduct of honey that is bottled as a crunchy, golden powder supplement. A little bitter and a little sweet, it is a balance of carbohydrates, fat and protein, all of which help to stimulate metabolism and fat burning, as well as protect against bad cholesterol. Buzzing with vitamins and minerals, it is also known as a hay fever cure — though it does come with a warning of anaphylaxis, which is an allergic reaction in some (especially those allergic to bee stings).

Summer Berries Breakfast Bowl

THIS ONE'S PERFECT FOR SUMMER DAYS OR HOLIDAYS, SERVED
AL FRESCO ON THE BALCONY OR PATIO. AND RELAX...

SERVES 2

SMOOTHIES

1 cup (125g, 4oz) mixed
summer berries, frozen

1 tbsp chia seeds

1 cup (250ml, 8fl oz)
almond milk

2 ripe bananas, peeled
and frozen

1 mango, chopped

2 tbsps macadamias

TOPPINGS

6 strawberries

¼ cup (30g, 1oz)
raspberries

2 passionfruit

$^1/_3$ cup (40g, 1½ oz)
hazelnuts, chopped

2 tbsps oats

Place summer berries, chia seeds and almond milk into a blender
and process until smooth.

Separately, place the mango, banana and macadamia into the
blender and process until smooth.

Pour the berry smoothie mix first into two bowls, then top with
the macadamia puree. Finish with the suggested toppings, or
toppings of your choice.

Dark Chocolate Quinoa Breakfast Bowl

FOR THOSE SLOW-MOVING MORNINGS WHEN YOU NEED AN ENERGY BOOST TO GET THE DAY STARTED: YOU CAN DO IT!

SERVES 3-4

1 cup (170g, 6oz) uncooked red and white quinoa, rinsed and strained

1 cup (250ml, 8fl oz) soy milk, plus more for serving

1 cup (250ml, 8fl oz) coconut water

Pinch of sea salt

2 tbsps raw cacao powder

2–3 tbsps maple syrup

¼ cup (40g, 1½ oz) dark chocolate, roughly chopped

TO SERVE

½ cup (60g, 2oz) hazelnuts, halved

1 cup (125g, 4oz) pecans

¼ cup (40g, 1½ oz) dark chocolate, shaved and roughly chopped

¼ cup (20g, ¾ oz) desiccated coconut

Place the quinoa, soy milk, coconut water and salt in a medium-sized saucepan and bring to the boil. Reduce the heat to low and simmer for 20 minutes, or until the quinoa is cooked.

Place the quinoa in a mixing bowl and stir through the cacao powder, maple syrup and dark chocolate. Add more or less of the cacao, syrup and chocolate, according to your taste.

Finish with the suggested toppings, or toppings of your choice.

Matcha Chia Pudding

SERVES 2

2 cups (500ml, 1pt) almond milk

4 tsps honey

1 tsp culinary grade matcha powder

Pinch of salt

6 tbsps chia seeds

Strawberries, to finish

Mint leaves, to garnish

Place almond milk, honey, matcha and salt in a jar with a secure lid and shake well to combine.

Place chia seeds in a bowl and pour the matcha almond milk over the top. Stir to combine and then cover with plastic wrap. Transfer to the fridge to chill.

After 15 minutes, remove from fridge and stir well, then return to fridge for 4 hours or more.

Serve with fresh strawberries and a couple of mint leaves.

Matcha Green Tea Brownie

SERVES 10

250g (9oz) unsalted butter, melted

1½ cups (235g, 8oz) white chocolate chips, melted

2 eggs

¼ cup (30g, 1oz) matcha green tea powder

½ cup (180g, 6oz) agave syrup

¾ cup (90g, 3oz) almond meal

1 cup (125g, 4oz) flour

¼ tsp vanilla extract

¼ cup (40g, 1½ oz) icing sugar substitute (stevia or xylitol)

Mint leaves, to garnish

Preheat oven to 180°C (350°F, Gas Mark 4). Grease and flour a baking tin.

Pour melted butter and chocolate into the bowl of an electric mixer. Allow to cool for 2–3 minutes then add eggs and matcha powder and beat on low until combined. Add flour, almond meal, agave and vanilla extract and mix until just incorporated. Pour batter into prepared pan and spread top with a spatula. Place in oven and bake for 20 minutes until firm to the touch. Remove from the oven and place tin on a wire rack to cool. Sift over the icing sugar substitute and garnish with mint leaves.

MATCHA TEA

In Japan, matcha tea is given as a gift, like a bottle of wine or bouquet of flowers. Matcha is the velvety, spearmint-green powder extracted from the leaves of green tea and now frothed up into lattes and sprinkled over breakfast cereal in trendy cafes. It tastes earthy and a little herby and is as caffeinated as coffee without the jittery effect. The leaves are high in antioxidants, including the potent catechin (pronounced 'cat-e-kin'), which boosts metabolism and helps the body process fats and sugars. Matcha also contains an amino acid called L-theanine, which stimulates relaxation without drowsiness.

ACAI

Acai is a gorgeous tropical berry that turns smoothies bright purple. It is even more purple than a blueberry, and bursting with even more fibre and 'super' qualities that keep the digestive system and circulation flowing smoothly. Acai berries are also high in anthocyanins, an antioxidant that balances cholesterol levels. Acai bowls are everywhere, usually made with frozen puree that's mostly sweet and a little bit sour and shouldn't come with added sugar. It's also available as a powder, which is best bought organic and with no additives. Check the labels!

Acai Super Smoothie Bowl

SERVES 1

1 banana (frozen or fresh)

½ cup (125ml, 4fl oz) coconut water

1 cup (250g, 9oz) plain yoghurt

1 x 100g (3½ oz) pkt frozen acai pulp (or 6 tbsps powdered acai)

2 cups (200g, 7oz) blueberries (frozen)

2 tbsps honey

1 tsp vanilla extract

1 cup (150g, 5oz) ice cubes

TO SERVE

2 tsps chia seeds

2 tsps bee pollen

Add all the ingredients to the blender and process until smooth enough to drink.

Pour into bowl and top with chia seeds and pollen or toppings of your choice.

Acai Berry Smoothie

SERVES 2

1 large banana

¾ cup (200ml, 6fl oz) coconut water

1 cup (250g, 9oz) plain yoghurt

1 x 100g (3½ oz) pkt frozen acai pulp (or 6 tbsps powdered acai)

1 cup (100g, 3½ oz) blueberries (frozen)

2 tbsps honey

1 tsp vanilla extract

1 cup (150g, 5oz) ice cubes

TOPPINGS

2 strawberries, halved

1 tbsp coconut flakes

2 tsps buckwheat

1 tbsp goji berries

1 tsp black chia seeds

Violet flowers, to garnish

Add all the smoothie ingredients to the blender and process until smooth enough to drink. Pour into serving glasses.

Finish with the suggested toppings, or toppings of your choice.

Overnight Oat and Chia Pudding

THIS SUBSTANTIAL AND CREAMY BREAKFAST PUDDING IS DESIGNED FOR EASE. MAKE THE NIGHT BEFORE AND IT'S READY TO GO

SERVES 2

PUDDING

½ cup (40g, 1½ oz) rolled oats

2 tbsps chia seeds

1½ cups (375ml, 13fl oz) soy milk

2 tbsps shredded coconut

2 tsps maple syrup

Pinch of cinnamon

Pinch of nutmeg

1 banana, mashed

TOPPINGS

1 tbsp honey

½ cup (60g, 2oz) pecans

In a small bowl, mix all the pudding ingredients except the banana. Leave in the fridge overnight.

In the morning, stir the banana through the pudding mix.

Top with the pecans and honey or with toppings of your choice.

Note: The maple syrup and honey in this pudding may be too much for some low sugar diets. Substitute the topping with fresh berries if preferred.

Grain-Free Muesli

JAM-PACKED WITH SUPER SEEDS AND UP-AND-AT-EM NUTS AND
BERRIES — YOU'LL BE GO GO GO WITH THIS FOR BREAKFAST

SERVES 10

3 cups (375g, 13oz)
mixed walnuts, almonds
and cashews

¼ cup (30g, 1oz) goji
berries

¼ cup (45g, 1½ oz)
dried apricots

¼ cup (45g, 1½ oz)
dates

½ cup (65g, 2oz)
pepitas (pumpkin
seeds)

1 cup (90g, 3oz)
desiccated coconut

2 tbsps maple syrup

3 tbsps honey

1 tbsp vanilla extract

½ tsp cinnamon

2 tsps sesame seeds

1 tbsp coconut oil

1-2 tbsps chia seeds

2 tsps poppyseeds

TO SERVE

Almond milk

Fresh strawberries

Fresh raspberries

Fresh blueberries

Goji berries

Preheat oven to 160°C (325°F, Gas Mark 3). Line a large flat
baking tray with baking paper.

Place the nuts and dried fruit in a food processor. Pulse several
times until the mixture starts to resemble rough breadcrumbs.
Remove the mix and place into a large bowl.

Add the pepitas, coconut, syrup, honey, vanilla, cinnamon,
sesame seeds and coconut oil.

Mix it all thoroughly, removing as many lumps as you can. (But
leave a few for the extra crunch!)

Spread it as evenly as possible over the baking tray.

Bake for 10 minutes, then remove from oven and mix everything
up. Bake for a further 10 minutes then mix it up again. Then
bake for a final 6 minutes.

Remove from the oven and let it dry out and cool to room
temperature. Stir through the chia and poppyseeds.

This will keep for up to 2 weeks in an airtight container in the
fridge.

Serve with almond milk and berries to taste.

Breakfast Polenta with Greek Yoghurt and Raspberries

A - HA! SOMETHING DIFFERENT AND DELICIOUS: THIS IS A FRESH NEW WAY TO EAT POLENTA THAT EVERYONE WILL ENJOY

SERVES 4

3 cups (750ml, 1 pt 9fl oz) water

1 cup (250ml, 8fl oz) orange juice

1 cup (160g, 6oz) coarse polenta

Pinch of salt

2 tbsps honey

1 cup (250g, 9oz) Greek yoghurt

1 cup (125g, 4oz) raspberries (fresh or frozen)

2 tsps maple syrup

Extra honey and mint leaves, to garnish

Bring the water and orange juice to a boil in a medium-sized saucepan.

Quickly stir in the salt, polenta and honey. Once it boils again, reduce the heat to low and cook for 30 minutes or until the polenta has softened. You need to stir this almost constantly to ensure there are no lumps. Add more water as needed.

To make the yoghurt topping, blend together the yoghurt, 1 tablespoon raspberries and the maple syrup until smooth.

Serve the hot polenta topped with a dollop of the raspberry yoghurt and extra raspberries. Garnish with a dollop of honey and fresh mint leaves

Tip: Wash the pot you cooked the polenta in immediately after use. The small amounts of cooked polenta left in the pot will harden to a cement-like consistency once cooled!

Almond and Pumpkin Breakfast Porridge

A WARMING AND GENTLY SPICY BREAKFAST DISH THAT'S PACKED FULL OF GOODNESS AND HOME COMFORT

SERVES 2

1 cup (225g, 8oz) butternut pumpkin, cooked and pureed

1/3 cup (85g, 3oz) almond butter (optional)

2 tbsps white chia seeds

1 cup (250ml, 8fl oz) almond milk

Pinch of sea salt

¼ tsp vanilla extract

½ tsp cinnamon

¼ tsp nutmeg

TOPPINGS

2 tbsps dried apricots, chopped

1 tbsp cacao nibs

¼ cup (30g, 1oz) chopped toasted walnuts

Mix together the pumpkin, chia seeds, ¾ cup almond milk, sea salt, vanilla extract, cinnamon and nutmeg in a saucepan.

Heat until boiling, then reduce the heat to low and cook, stirring frequently, for 5 minutes.

Stir in almond butter, if using. Let sit for 10 minutes to cool.

Serve with the rest of the almond milk and the toppings sprinkled over, or the toppings of your choice.

DETOX WITH WATER

Eight glasses of water a day. It's a well-known fact that is actually a bit of a myth. It turns out we should drink when we're thirsty — no more, no less. However, drinking enough to quench our thirst is essential. Water keeps bones and bodies hydrated, obviously. It balances our body temperature and also helps flush toxins and byproducts of fats and sugars from our kidneys and liver. And it fills up the body so that we crave fewer sugary things. If the belly is filled with water, it's easier to forget about that sneaky can of soft drink in the fridge.

And the earlier in the day, the better. A glass of warm water with fresh lemon juice in the morning gets the metabolism firing and balances the digestive system for the day. The lemon sets the body's chemistry on an even keel and slowly, those cravings for chocolate at 10am or for cake in the middle of the night should dissolve.

And before every meal, try drinking half a glass of water. This will fill the belly up and lower hunger levels, making it easier to eat slowly and moderately.

It sounds too easy. What makes it even easier: flavours! Avoid bottled 'natural' flavoured waters, which are likely to contain either sugar or preservatives. It's easy to create your own water infused with fresh fruit, vegetables and fresh herbs.

SIMPLE COMBINATIONS

LEMON, LIME AND CUCUMBER: Slice lemons, limes and peeled cucumber. The cucumber adds an earthiness to the sour fruit.

ORANGE, RASPBERRIES AND GINGER: Slice unpeeled oranges and toss with whole or muddled raspberries. Finely grate in a little ginger for zing. The orange rind adds a sour twist and the flesh of the raspberries will give occasional sweet bites.

STRAWBERRIES AND MINT: Wash and rub the mint gently between the hands to release the full flavour, then mix with a big handful of sliced strawberries. This drink tastes like it has sneaky sugar in it.

DIY TIPS

Fill jugs with filtered water. It's best to prepare a whole jug so the water is ready when thirst strikes. Keep them in the fridge and the longer they infuse, the stronger the flavour.

Consider 'muddling'. A mortar and pestle or potato masher will work to mash up the fruit flesh, releasing the juice and enriching the water with sweet fleshy mouthfuls.

Sparkling water is a great alternative to still water.

Black Rice and Pomegranate Salad Bowl

DON'T SKIMP ON THE POMEGRANATE — IT'S THOUGHT TO BOAST ONE OF THE RICHEST COMBINATIONS OF ANTIOXIDANTS OF ALL FRUIT AND VEG

SERVES 2

SALAD

2 large pomegranates, seeded

3 cups (90g, 3oz) baby spinach leaves

1 cup (155g, 4oz) black rice

1 cup (125g, 4oz) toasted walnuts

1 cup (110g, 4oz) Greek feta cheese, chopped

DRESSING

3 tbsps olive oil

2 tbsps lemon juice

2 tbsps maple syrup

1 tbsp apple cider vinegar

¼ tsp Dijon mustard

Pinch of salt and pepper

To cook the rice, rinse well and place in a medium-sized pot. Cover with 3 cups of cold water. Cover and bring to the boil. Reduce heat to low and simmer, covered, for 20 minutes, or until the rice is tender.

To make the dressing, whisk together all the dressing ingredients in a small bowl, pour into a serving jug and set aside.

To serve, layer the serving plates with the spinach leaves, then place a portion of the rice on top.

Place portions of the remaining ingredients over the top.

Serve with the dressing.

Cheesy Polenta with Pesto and Roasted Spicy Chickpeas

CRUNCHY CHICKPEAS PROVIDE THE PERFECT COMPLEMENT TO CREAMY POLENTA IN THIS WINTER WARMER

SERVES 4

POLENTA

2 tbsps unsalted butter

1 clove garlic, crushed

5 cups (1.25L, 42fl oz) vegetable stock

1 tsp salt flakes

1½ cups (240g, 8oz) polenta

1 cup (250ml, 8fl oz) soy or almond milk

1 cup (125g, 4oz) tasty cheese, grated

¼ cup (25g, 1oz) Parmesan cheese, grated

Salt and pepper, to taste

BASIL MACADAMIA PESTO

2 cups (90g, 3oz) packed fresh basil leaves

½ cup (60g, 2oz) macadamia nuts

3 cloves garlic, chopped

¼ cup (25g, 1oz) Parmesan cheese, grated

½ cup (125ml, 4fl oz) olive oil

CHICKPEAS

1 x 400g (14oz) can chickpeas, drained, rinsed

½ tsp salt

2 tsps sweet paprika

1½ tsps ground cumin

2 tsps mild curry powder

To make the spicy chickpeas, preheat oven to 170°C (340°F, Gas Mark 4) and line a baking tray with baking paper.

Place chickpeas on prepared tray. Sieve the spices over the top and toss to coat. Ensure even coating of the chickpeas.

Roast chickpeas for 1 hour or until golden and crispy. Then cool chickpeas on baking tray.

To make the pesto, place the basil leaves, macadamia nuts, garlic and Parmesan in a blender. Pulse a few times to mix everything together. Then add the oil in small amounts, blending as you go until it becomes a thick, grainy paste. Season to taste.

To make the polenta, heat the butter in a medium saucepan over medium heat. Add the garlic and sauté for 2 minutes. Add the stock and bring to a boil.

Quickly stir in the salt, polenta and milk. Once it boils again, reduce the heat to low and cook for 30 minutes or until the polenta has softened.

You need to stir this almost constantly to ensure there are no lumps. Add more stock as needed. Once the polenta is cooked, stir in the cheeses and season to taste. Let cool for 5 minutes before serving.

To serve, place equal portions of the polenta onto your serving plates. Top with a handful of spicy chickpeas and a dessertspoon or two of the pesto.

Bacon and Cheese Stuffed Omelette

A LIGHT AND EASY BREAKFAST FOR TWO THAT CAN BE MADE IN MINUTES

SERVES 2

6 eggs

¹/₃ cup (80ml, 3fl oz) milk

125g (4oz) butter

4 slices bacon, rinds removed

1 cup (125g, 4oz) cheddar cheese, grated

1 spring onion, finely sliced

Basil leaves, to garnish

In a large jug, whisk together eggs and milk. Season to taste.

Melt half the butter in a frying pan over a medium-high heat. Fry the bacon for 5 minutes or until cooked to your preference. Drain the cooked bacon on paper towels.

Add the remaining butter to the frying pan and reduce the heat to medium.

Add half the egg mixture. When almost set, sprinkle over half the cheese and layer over 2 slices of bacon. Fold over and cook for 1 minute. Slide onto a serving plate.

Repeat previous step with the remaining ingredients for the second omelette.

To serve, sprinkle omelettes with spring onions, and basil leaves for garnish.

Green Scrambled Eggs

A FRESH AND BRIGHT BREAKFAST THAT WILL HELP
YOU GET THE DAY OFF TO A HAPPY START

SERVES 2

4 eggs

¼ cup (60ml, 2fl oz) milk

Salt and pepper, to season

55g (2oz) Greek feta cheese, finely cubed

2 tsps butter

2 tbsps chives, chopped

¼ cup (7g, ¼ oz) baby spinach leaves, finely chopped

2 radishes, quartered and sliced

Lightly beat eggs, milk and a pinch of salt and pepper in a bowl until loosely mixed. Allow a few strands of white or yolk to remain. Drop cubes of feta into the mixture.

Heat butter in large frying pan over a medium heat until just sizzling. Pour in the egg mixture.

Leave to cook undisturbed for 10–15 seconds then as the eggs begin to set, gently draw the eggs across the pan with an inverted spatula or wooden spoon. Repeat a few times until large soft curds form. Don't stir and don't overcook.

Remove from the heat and gently mix through the chives and spinach.

Serve topped with radish.

PROTEIN, THE SUGAR WARRIOR

Sugar cravings are tricky. Sugar in all its forms — from berries and fresh orange juice to ice cream and those sneaky lollies rolling around the handbag — is a taste most of us have come to love. And the cravings are chemical: our brains are predisposed to love sugar, making it hard to just say no.

Life without any sugar at all perhaps isn't necessary, but reducing sugar intake can be transformative. And the key is to train the body — our seemingly natural receptivity to sugar can be rewired. There are many tricks: the main one is to fill the body with food that satisfies both the taste buds and energy levels. Along with fibre and fat, protein is a warrior that gives us strength and helps us fight the 'war' on sugar cravings.

Research shows that protein in the morning, for example, makes it harder for sugar cravings to have you in their clutches later on. High protein foods produce less of the hunger-stimulating hormone ghrelin, and more PPY, a hormone that signals fullness. MRI scans have shown reduced craving activity in the brain after breakfasts of yoghurt, eggs and cheese.

Plain Greek yoghurt contains healthy doses of fat and is high in protein. For a simple breakfast, stir chia seeds — which transform in liquid into smooth, chewy protein bursts — into a bowl of yoghurt. Maybe add a squirt of raw honey.

The queen of high protein breakfasts is eggs. No longer considered a cholesterol villain, an egg or even three a day is a great answer to the question 'what's for breakfast?'. Eggs deliver B vitamins and omega-3 'good fats' as well as iron for bones.

TIPS

Boil up eggs on a Sunday night and have a quick breakfast ready to go. Crack one open, season with salt and pepper or dip into a bowl of hummus, and eat with your hands.

Huevos rancheros are brunch magic. For a light and scrumptious version of the Mexican dish, top poached eggs with pureed black beans, avocado and a spicy tomato sauce. Use lots of fresh parsley as a garnish, and Parmesan is a high protein cheesy topping. (Or indulge in a dollop of sour cream… because that's the way the pros do it.)

Become the master or mistress of the scrambled egg. Some recipes suggest a dash of cream in the beaten eggs. Others add cheese. Either way: use free-range eggs and beat lightly just before throwing in the pan, which should be on low heat. Use butter in the pan — it adds flavour, cream and nutrients. Garnish with salt and pepper.

Quinoa Basil Salad with Poached Egg

KEEP YOURSELF FUELLED UP AND READY TO RUMBLE WITH THIS SUPERFOOD-FILLED BREAKFAST OPTION

SERVES 2

PESTO

1 bunch (80g, 3oz) basil, chopped

3 cloves garlic

5 tbsps olive oil

¼ cup (25g, 1oz) Parmesan cheese, grated

2 tbsps water

2 tbsps lemon juice

½ cup (40g, 1½ oz) walnuts, chopped

1 tsp salt

Pinch of pepper

QUINOA

1 cup (170g, 6oz) red and white quinoa

2 cups (500ml, 1pt) vegetable stock

¼ cup (10g, ¼ oz) parsley leaves, chopped

2 poached eggs

Place the quinoa and stock in a small saucepan and bring to the boil. Reduce the heat to low and simmer for 20 minutes, or until the quinoa is cooked.

Put all the pesto ingredients apart from the walnuts and oil into a food processor. Pulse a couple of times. Add half the walnuts and the oil and pulse until the walnuts are roughly broken up and incorporated into the pesto and it's a rough paste. Taste and add more seasoning if necessary. Set aside.

Stir about 2 tablespoons of pesto through the quinoa until coated. Add more pesto to taste. Warm on a low heat for 1–2 minutes to warm the pesto. Toss the chopped parsley and remaining walnuts through the quinoa.

To serve, separate the quinoa into two serving bowls and top each with a poached egg.

Home-Style Fried Eggs with Chilli Sauce

HOT, SPICY, CRUNCHY AND FIESTY. THIS ASIAN-STYLE BREAKFAST OPTION WILL GET ALL SYSTEMS FIRING

SERVES 4

CHILLI SAUCE (MAKES 1 CUP)

8 large red chillies, roughly chopped

3 tbsps ginger, chopped

1 clove garlic, chopped

½ cup (125ml, 4fl oz) peanut oil

2 tsps palm sugar

2 tbsps tamari

4 tbsps chilli sauce

1 cup (250ml, 8fl oz) canola or vegetable oil

8 eggs

¼ tsp white pepper

2 springs onion, sliced

1 large red chilli, seeds removed, thinly sliced

Fresh coriander, to garnish

To make the chilli sauce, place the chillies, ginger and garlic in a blender or food processor and blend until mixed to a paste.

Heat the oil in a wok or frying pan over medium-high heat. Add the chilli paste and stir-fry for 2 minutes. Add the palm sugar and tamari and stir for 1 minute

Reduce the heat to low and let it cook for 10 minutes. The oil may separate out from the paste — just stir it back through.

To make the eggs, heat the oil in a wok or frying pan over medium-high heat.

Working quickly, crack each egg, one at a time, into a small bowl, then gently tip the egg into the oil. Let them fry for 1 minute.

Reduce the heat to low and cook them for another minute or until the bottoms of the eggs are crispy and cooked, but the yolks are still runny.

Use a large slotted spoon to scoop up the eggs then drain the oil from the wok. Return the eggs to the wok and keep cooking for 30 seconds or until they're crisp.

Remove the eggs and briefly drain on paper towels. Serve the eggs hot, seasoned with pepper and garnished with chilli sauce, spring onion, sliced chilli and coriander.

White Bean and Carrot Hummus Tartlets with Coriander Pesto

TRY SOMETHING NEW: THESE ELEGANT TARTLETS ARE ORIGINAL, PRETTY AND FULL OF DELICATE FLAVOURS

MAKES 18

PESTO

2 cups (90g, 3oz) packed fresh coriander leaves

¼ cup (35g, 1¼ oz) pine nuts

3 cloves garlic, chopped

¼ cup (25g, 1oz) Parmesan cheese, grated

½ cup (125ml, 4fl oz) olive oil

3 tbsps pine nuts, to garnish

HUMMUS

2 carrots, peeled and chopped

1 x 400g (14oz) can cannellini beans, drained and rinsed

1 clove garlic, minced

½ tsp of salt

2 tbsps tahini

2 tbsps of lemon juice

2 tsps lemon zest

¼ tsp cayenne pepper

TARTLETS

1 cup (125g, 4oz) plain flour

1 cup (125g, 4oz) ground buckwheat flour

125g (4oz) butter

Pinch of salt

⅓ cup (80ml, 3fl oz) chilled water

To make the pesto, place the coriander leaves, pine nuts, garlic and Parmesan in a blender. Pulse a few times to mix everything together. Then add the oil in small amounts, blending as you go until it becomes a thick, grainy paste. Season to taste.

To make the hummus, boil the carrots in lightly salted water for 12 minutes until tender. Drain and place in a food processor. Add the beans, garlic, salt, tahini, lemon juice, zest and cayenne and blend until smooth. Season to taste.

To make the tartlets, place the flours, salt and butter in a food processor and pulse until the mixture looks like breadcrumbs. Add the cold water in small amounts and pulse one or two times until the pastry starts to come together. Don't add more water than you need to.

Take out of the processor and knead for a minute or two on a lightly floured surface until the pastry is smooth. Shape it into a round ball and flatten slightly into a disc shape. Wrap in plastic wrap and place in the fridge for 30 minutes.

Preheat oven to 180°C (350°F, Gas Mark 4). Lightly oil then flour tartlet moulds or 6-hole large muffin tins.

Roll out the dough to a thickness of 2mm. Try not to handle the dough too much or it will become hard.

Cut out circles large enough to fit into the moulds and come up the sides. Push the pastry into the moulds and fill each tartlet case with a layer of foil, then some baking beads or rice.

Bake for 10 minutes. Remove from oven and remove the foil and beads. Place 2 tablespoons of hummus into the tarts and bake for a further 15 minutes, until the tartlet edges are golden.

Repeat with the remaining pastry and filling. Serve with a small spoonful of pesto on top and a couple of pine nuts to garnish.

Everyday Lunches

Cauliflower Sandwiches

SERVES 4

2 large red capsicums, quartered and seeded

2 tbsps olive oil

1 large head cauliflower, broken into small florets

½ cup (75g, 3oz) grated potato, squeezed to remove excess liquid

2 medium onions, chopped

2 tbsps wholemeal flour

2 cloves garlic, chopped

1 tsp Vegemite or other yeast extract spread

2 tsps fresh oregano leaves, finely chopped

1 tbsp fresh parsley leaves, finely chopped

1 tsp lemon juice

½ cup (60g, 2oz) tasty cheese, grated

2 large eggs, lightly beaten

¼ cup (60ml, 2fl oz) olive oil

300g (10oz) mozzarella, sliced

Salt and pepper

Preheat oven to 220°C (430°F, Gas Mark 7). Line a large flat baking tray with baking paper.

Place the capsicum quarters on the tray and drizzle over with the olive oil.

Bake in the oven for at least 25 minutes, or until they start to blacken and the skin blisters.

Remove from the oven and seal them in a plastic bag for 15 minutes. Once they are cool enough to handle, peel off the skins and cut the skin into 2cm-thick (1in) slices. Set aside.

Boil the cauliflower in a pot of lightly salted water for 5 minutes, or until tender. Drain the florets and place in a food processor along with the potato, onion, flour, garlic, Vegemite, oregano, parsley, lemon juice, cheese and eggs.

Blend until the mix is smooth and thick. Form into 8 large flat patties.

Heat half the olive oil in a large frying pan until shimmering. Reduce heat slightly. Fry each pattie for 4 minutes then flip over. Place a slice or two of mozzarella on top of half of the fritters and a couple of slices of the roast capsicum. Cook for a further 4 minutes.

Carefully remove from the pan and top with another cooked fritter. Season to taste. Slice in half and serve hot.

Quinoa and Pumpkin Gratin

A COMFORTING AND NUTRITIOUS DISH THAT WILL
HAPPILY FILL HUNGRY BELLIES

SERVES 4

1 cup (170g, 6oz) red
and white quinoa

2½ cups (625ml, 1pt
5fl oz) vegetable stock

2 tbsps olive oil

2 large onions, chopped

3 cloves garlic, minced

700g (1½ lb) butternut
pumpkin, diced

1 tbsp fresh Thai basil
leaves, chopped

1 tbsp fresh rosemary,
chopped

3 large eggs, lightly
beaten

½ cup (60g, 2oz) Swiss
cheese, grated

¼ cup (25g, 1oz)
Parmesan cheese,
grated

½ cup (70g, 2½ oz) plus
2 tbsps pine nuts

Salt and freshly ground
pepper

Extra Thai basil leaves,
to garnish

Place the quinoa and 2 cups of the stock in a small saucepan
and bring to the boil. Reduce the heat to low and simmer for 20
minutes, or until the quinoa is cooked. Set aside.

Heat the oil in a large saucepan over medium-high heat. Add
the onion and garlic and sauté for 5 minutes, until the onion is
translucent. Add the pumpkin, basil and rosemary and fry for
3 minutes. Add the rest of the stock, turn the heat to low, cover
and cook for 12 minutes, or until the pumpkin has softened.
Remove from the heat and let cool for 15 minutes.

Preheat the oven to 190°C (375°F, Gas Mark 5). Lightly oil a
medium-sized casserole dish.

Place the quinoa, pumpkin mixture, eggs, Swiss cheese, ½ cup
of pine nuts and a good couple of grinds of salt and pepper in a
large mixing bowl and stir to combine thoroughly.

Place in the casserole dish and sprinkle over the Parmesan and
remaining pine nuts.

Bake for 40 minutes until the cheese is golden brown and
bubbling on top.

Let cool for 10 minutes before serving.

Garnish with a couple of basil leaves.

Cabbage and Sausage Strudel

THIS TANGY, SALTY STRUDEL IS FULL OF FLAVOUR. SERVE
A SLICE AS IT IS OR WITH A BIG GREEN SALAD FOR LUNCH

SERVES 8

1.2kg (2½ lb) green
cabbage, cored and
shredded

1 medium onion,
quartered and sliced

2 tbsps salt flakes

¼ cup (60ml, 2fl oz)
olive oil

1 tbsp apple cider
vinegar

200g (7oz) kransky
sausage, chopped

1 small red capsicum,
seeded and chopped

1½ tsps maple syrup

Salt and freshly ground
pepper

8 sheets filo pastry

¾ cup (170g, 6oz)
butter, melted

1 tbsp caraway seeds

Mix the cabbage, onion and salt together in a large plastic colander
(don't use metal). Let it sit for 2 hours to let the salt draw out the liquid.
Push out as much liquid as you can and pat dry the vegetables with
paper towels.

Heat the olive oil in a large high-sided frying pan over medium heat.
Add the cabbage, vinegar, kransky, capsicum and maple syrup. Sauté for
20 minutes until the cabbage has softened and is tender.

Season to taste and let the mixture cool for 20 minutes.

Preheat oven to 190°C (375°F, Gas Mark 5). Line a long flat baking tray
with lightly oiled baking paper.

Place one sheet of filo on a lightly oiled flat work surface. Lightly brush
with the melted butter. Place another sheet on top and again lightly
brush with the melted butter. Repeat with the remaining filo sheets.

Spoon the cabbage mix all along one of the longer edges of the filo
sheets, leaving a 2cm (1in) gap along the edge. Make the mix about 7cm
(3in) wide.

Carefully roll up the filo from the edge closest to the mixture. Place the
rolled-up strudel on the baking tray, seam side down.

Brush any remaining butter on the top and sprinkle with caraway seeds.

Bake in the oven for 35 minutes, until golden.

Home-Made Mayonnaise

MAKES 1 CUP

1 large egg yolk

1½ tsps fresh lemon juice

1 tsp white wine vinegar

¼ tsp Dijon mustard

½ tsp salt

½ tsp freshly ground black pepper

¾ cup (185ml, 6fl oz) olive oil

Whisk together the egg yolk, lemon juice, vinegar, mustard, salt and pepper until blended and bright yellow.

Gradually add a quarter of the olive oil and whisk by hand for 4 minutes.

Whisk in the remaining oil gradually, until the mayonnaise thickens to the desired consistency. This may take 10 minutes.

If the mixture looks like it's about to separate, stop adding the oil and briskly whisk until it forms a creamy mix again. Then continue adding the oil.

Cover and refrigerate. Keep chilled before serving.

Orange Poppy-Seed Dressing

MAKES 1 CUP

½ cup (125ml, 4fl oz) orange juice

¼ cup (90g, 3oz) maple syrup

¼ cup (60ml, 2fl oz) avocado oil

2 tbsps apple cider vinegar

1 tsp poppyseeds

Salt and freshly ground pepper

Place all the dressing ingredients together in a small bowl.

Whisk vigorously until everything is combined.

Season to taste with salt and pepper.

The mixture will start to separate if left to sit for too long.

Give it a quick whisk again just before serving.

BALSAMIC VINEGAR

The pungent, sweet, dark, shiny vinegar is something of a miracle substance — it lasts forever (almost), can save any salad (with the help of a little olive oil) and does wonders for the body. In Italy, balsamic vinegar is made from grape juice that is fermented and traditionally aged for at least 12 years. The polyphenols help balance out bad cholesterol and the vinegar's sweetness is low in glucose, so will not cause artificial blood sugar spikes, unless guzzled in big doses (it's tasty but that would be extreme!).

Buckwheat and Roast Cauliflower Salad

THIS HEARTY AND HEALTHY SALAD IS PACKED FULL OF GOODNESS AND ENERGY - BOOSTING NUTRIENTS

SERVES 4

1 cup (170g, 6oz) buckwheat groats

2 cups (500ml, 1pt) vegetable stock

2 cups (650g, 1lb 6oz) cauliflower florets, cut in halves

2 red capsicums, quartered and seeded

3 tbsps olive oil

1 tsp ground cumin

1 tsp ground oregano

2 cloves garlic, minced

1 large red onion, quartered and sliced

¾ cup (35g, 1¼ oz) fresh parsley leaves, chopped

½ cup (20g, ¾ oz) basil leaves, roughly chopped

2 preserved lemon quarters, finely chopped

Salt and freshly ground pepper

Olive oil, to serve

1 small lemon, cut into wedges, to garnish

Preheat oven to 220°C (430°F, Gas Mark 7). Line a large flat baking tray with baking paper.

Place the stock and buckwheat in a large saucepan and bring to the boil. Reduce the heat to low and simmer, covered, for 20 minutes, until the buckwheat is tender.

Remove from the heat and set aside to cool.

In a large bowl, toss the cauliflower florets and capsicum quarters with the olive oil. Remove the capsicum quarters and lay them out on the baking tray, skin side up.

Add the cumin, oregano, garlic and onion slices to the cauliflower and toss through again.

Bake the capsicum in the oven for at least 25 minutes, or until the skins start to blacken and the skin blisters. Remove from the oven and seal the capsicum in a plastic bag for 15 minutes.

Spread the cauliflower and onion on the baking tray. Reduce the heat to 200°C (400°F, Gas Mark 6) and roast the vegetables for 30 minutes, until browned, turning them halfway through.

Once the capsicum is cool enough to handle, peel off the skins and cut the skin into 2cm (1in) cubes.

Place the buckwheat, fresh herbs, preserved lemon, cauliflower mix and capsicum in a large bowl and toss to combine. Season to taste.

Serve warm with lemon wedges and some olive oil drizzled over.

Superfoods Salad

THE CLUE IS IN THE TITLE: THIS BRIGHT AND CRUNCHY SALAD IS SUPER TASTY, SUPER EASY AND SUPER GOOD FOR YOU

SERVES 4

SALAD

½ cup (100g, 3½ oz) pearl barley

½ cup (85g, 3oz) red quinoa

3 cups (750ml, 1 pt 9fl oz) vegetable stock

2 cups (200g, 7oz) small broccoli florets

½ cup (80g, 3oz) fresh peas

1 zucchini, halved and thinly sliced lengthways

2 tsps olive oil

Salt and freshly ground pepper

4 cups (280g, 10oz) kale, rinsed, stems removed and chopped

1 Lebanese cucumber, thinly sliced

¼ red cabbage, shredded

½ cup (60g, 2oz) walnuts, chopped

1 avocado, sliced

DRESSING

¼ cup (60ml, 2fl oz) grapefruit juice

1 tbsp maple syrup

2 tbsps olive oil

1 clove garlic, crushed

½ tsp sea salt

¼ tsp pepper, or to taste

1 tsp Greek yoghurt

1 tbsp fresh parsley, finely chopped

Place the barley and stock in a medium saucepan and bring to the boil. Reduce heat and simmer, covered, for 15 minutes. Stir the quinoa into the saucepan and continue simmering for 25 minutes, until the barley is tender and chewy. Fluff the barley and quinoa with a fork, remove from heat and set aside to cool, covered.

Bring a medium saucepan of lightly salted water to the boil. Boil the broccoli florets and peas for 2 minutes, then drain and set aside.

In a small bowl, gently toss the zucchini slices with olive oil and a couple of grinds of salt and pepper.

Heat a grill pan on medium-high heat. Grill the zucchini slices for 2 minutes on either side, or until light grill marks appear. Remove from heat and place in a large bowl.

Add the rest of the salad ingredients, except the avocado, to the zucchini and toss to combine. Then gently mix the avocado slices through the salad, trying not to break them up.

To make the dressing, whisk all the dressing ingredients together in a small bowl.

Serve the salad with the dressing on the side.

FREEKEH

Freekeh has a funny name and superstar qualities. Wheat that has been picked before ripening, it comes off the plant still soft and green, then it is roasted or sun-dried to a very light gold colour, often with tinges of the original green. The roasting retains most of the grains' nutrients and natural nuttiness, which makes it perfect in texture and taste to replace rice, pasta and even the 'super seed' quinoa.

It turns out, freekeh has about double the amount of protein and fibre as the same quantity of quinoa. It is also lower on the glycemic index (GI) than quinoa, which is the best thing! A food's GI measures the ways that carbohydrates convert to sugar. The higher the GI, the more intense the energy rush — and then the more intense the energy drop. The lower the GI, the more sustainable the energy will be. Foods with a low GI fill up bellies for longer and will lessen sweet cravings later.

So, freekeh is low in sugar, should lessen sugar cravings, and is packed with iron, calcium and zinc. One caveat: freekeh is not great news for those who are gluten intolerant — this is a wheat product.

Convinced? Now, start cooking.

Freekeh infuses any dish with a light smokiness and a herbal taste that is retained through the roasting, boiling and steaming process.

HOW TO COOK

The cracked grains are easier and quicker to cook than whole grains. Run freekeh under water until the water runs clear, then rub down with a paper towel. Bring to the boil in salted water, cover and simmer until water is absorbed — about 15 minutes for cracked grain and 45 minutes for whole grain. Watch the water levels so the grain doesn't fully dry out. Steam will lead to a fluffier bowl of freekeh. Remove from the heat and use a fork to fluff up.

FREEKEH FOR BREAKFAST: Substitute freekeh for oats and stir in yoghurt, peaches and cinnamon for a high-energy, scrumptious start to the day.

FREEKEH SALAD WITH SALMON: Lightly steam salmon fillets until silky. Cook freekeh to retain some crunch, then dress with a blend of olive oil, lemon juice and plain Greek yoghurt. Stir in dill, mint and parsley, then place salmon on top. This is a luxurious salad with triple doses of protein.

FREEKEH RISOTTO WITH BROCCOLINI: Lightly sauté broccolini and freekeh in olive oil, garlic, fennel seeds and pepper, then add stock. Simmer for up to 15 minutes. In a blender, mix ricotta cheese, basil leaves and lemon. Stir this through the freekeh. Serve with parsley and Parmesan.

Smoked Chicken and Sprout Salad

MUNG BEANS ARE A GOOD SOURCE OF, WELL, PRETTY MUCH
EVERYTHING. ENJOY THEM IN THIS FLAVOURSOME SALAD

SERVES 2-4

½ cup (90g, 3oz)
cracked freekeh, rinsed
and drained

1½ cups (375ml,
13fl oz) vegetable stock

2 large smoked chicken
breasts, cut into cubes

1 x 400g (14oz) can
cannellini beans, rinsed
and drained

2 cups (200g, 7oz)
sprouted mung beans,
rinsed

2 large tomatoes,
chopped

¼ cup (30g, 1oz)
sunflower seeds

½ cup (20g, ¾ oz) fresh
parsley leaves, chopped

2 tbsps dill, roughly
chopped

2 tbsps olive oil

1 tbsp apple cider
vinegar

1 tsp maple syrup

Salt and freshly ground
pepper

Sprigs of dill and
parsley, to garnish

Place the freekeh and stock in a small saucepan and bring to the
boil. Reduce the heat to low and simmer for 20 minutes, or until
the freekeh is cooked. Set aside to cool for 20 minutes

Place the rest of the salad ingredients, along with the freekeh, in
a large bowl. Toss to combine thoroughly.

Serve garnished with dill and parsley leaves.

Quinoa Stuffed Pumpkin

THIS VERSATILE FILLING ALSO WORKS WELL NESTLED
INTO HALVES OF EGGPLANT OR CAPSICUM

SERVES 4

2 small butternut pumpkins, halved lengthways and seeds scooped out

3 tbsps olive oil

Salt and freshly ground pepper

½ cup (85g, 3oz) quinoa

1½ cups (375ml, 13fl oz) vegetable stock

1 small onion, finely chopped

1 clove garlic, crushed

¼ cup (30g, 1oz) fresh breadcrumbs

¼ cup (25g, 1oz) Parmesan cheese

½ cup (55g, 2oz) Greek feta cheese, crumbled

½ tsp sea salt

1 tsp ground oregano

1 tsp ground cumin

1 tsp cinnamon

1 tbsp maple syrup

½ cup (20g, ¾ oz) fresh parsley leaves, chopped

4 sprigs parsley, to garnish

Preheat oven to 180°C (350°F, Gas Mark 5). Line a large flat baking tray with baking paper.

Place the pumpkin halves on the baking tray, cut side up. Drizzle over half the olive oil and a couple of good grinds of salt and pepper.

Bake for 30 minutes. Remove from oven and scoop out the inside, leaving a 1cm (½ in) layer of flesh. Mash the scooped-out pumpkin flesh and place in a large mixing bowl.

Place the quinoa and stock in a small saucepan and bring to the boil. Reduce the heat to low and simmer for 20 minutes, or until the quinoa is cooked.

Heat the rest of the oil in a small frying pan over medium heat. Add the onion and garlic and sauté for 5 minutes, until the onion is translucent.

Combine the onion mix, quinoa, breadcrumbs, Parmesan, feta, spices, salt, maple syrup and chopped parsley in the bowl with the pumpkin flesh.

Spoon the mixture into the pumpkin halves. Bake in the oven for 40 minutes, until the pumpkins are completely softened.

Serve warm, garnished with parsley leaves.

BURGERS WITHOUT BUNS

What's a burger without the bun? It's a healthy choice! A burger bun is not the worst carbohydrate-and-sugar offender, but cutting it out will eliminate around 20g of carbs and, depending on the bun, up to 10g of sugar. If the bun is white, factor in extra sugar from the carbohydrates, which the body converts into sugars. Whole-wheat buns with seeds are a better choice. They rate mid-range on the GI index — they might slow the digestion down a touch but they do pack extra nutrients. But why not use vegetables instead? It can be a delicious choice, and just takes a bit of imagination. The trick with faux burger buns is stability: the substitute needs to have a bit of gripping power, to hold the meat or the veggies inside for neat yet substantial bites.

THE BEST BUNS

EGGPLANT BUN: Choose a shiny purple 'globe' eggplant, which has a round, bulbous body. Cut into nice thick discs. Salt the discs for 30 minutes, then rinse. Drizzle in olive oil and season with salt and pepper, then bake for 20 minutes. Flip them halfway through and test — the flesh should get a little moist and silky but not mushy, or the burger will be slightly messy.

TASTE TIP: For a sauce, try hummus or tahini with lemon, delicious partners to eggplant.

SWEET POTATO BUN: Choose a sizable potato so that the discs are wide enough to hold at least a small burger patty. Do the olive oil drizzle, season with salt and pepper. Roast in the oven for 30 minutes, flipping halfway for tender but firm potato rounds.

TASTE TIP: Caramelized onions are naturally sweet and sandwich beautifully between the earthy sweet potato and the rich meat.

AVOCADO BUN: Scoop two halves of avocado from the skin. Slice the most rounded parts off to create a flat surface for easier gripping. Fill with a very thin burger patty or lightly fry bacon or halloumi instead. Add a crunchy lettuce leaf, salt and pepper.

TASTE TIP: Mix a side pot of tahini, plain yoghurt and lemon juice. Spread it on between bites.

PORTOBELLO MUSHROOM BUN: With this meaty, smoky, salty 'shroom, barely a burger is needed. Drizzle olive oil and barbecue or sauté the mushroom until it is quite soft. Give it at least 8 minutes, or it will be tough to chew into. Add a slim burger patty or bacon, and tomato and crunchy lettuce.

TASTE TIP: Feta or goat's cheese is a dreamy spread between mushroom and meat. Or skip the meat and make it a vegetarian delight.

Portobello Mushroom Burger

MAKE MUSHROOMS THE MAIN EVENT AT THE NEXT BURGER
NIGHT AT YOUR PLACE

SERVES 2

4 large portobello
mushrooms, wiped
clean and stems
removed

1 tbsp olive oil

1 tbsp tamari sauce

1 clove garlic, minced

1 tsp salt flakes

1 avocado

1 tsp lime juice

Salt and freshly ground
pepper

Handful mixed salad
leaves, washed and
dried

1 large tomato, cut into
thick slices

Mayonnaise (see recipe
page 72)

2 tsps sesame seeds

Preheat oven to 190°C (375°F, Gas Mark 5). Line a large flat
baking tray with baking paper.

Mix together the oil, tamari, garlic and salt flakes. Lightly coat
each mushroom in the mixture and place them upside down on
the baking tray.

Roast for 10 minutes, then turn them over and roast for a further
15 minutes.

Remove them from the tray and let them sit on paper towels to
help remove some of the excess liquid.

Mash the avocado together with the lime juice and salt and
pepper to taste.

To assemble, place two mushrooms upside down on your serving
plate. Spread half the avocado onto each mushroom.

Top with a slice or two of tomato, then some salad leaves, then a
good dollop of mayonnaise.

Top with the other mushroom half and sprinkle them with
sesame seeds.

Spinach and Tuna Quiche

THIS CLASSIC FLAVOUR COMBINATION PROVIDES A GREAT PROTEIN BOOST THAT IS EXCELLENT FOR LOW SUGAR DIETS

SERVES 6

PASTRY

1¾ cups (215g, 7oz) plain flour

125g (4oz) chilled butter, cut into cubes

1 egg yolk

2 tbsps chilled water

FILLING

1 tbsp olive oil

1 small leek, sliced

4 large eggs, lightly beaten

1 x 425g (15oz) can tuna, drained

150g (5oz) baby spinach, chopped

½ tsp salt

¼ tsp pepper

Preheat oven to 200°C (400°F, Gas Mark 6) and grease a 23cm (9in) quiche dish.

Place the flour and butter in a food processor and pulse until the mixture looks like breadcrumbs. Whisk together the egg yolk and cold water and add to the mixture. Pulse until the pastry starts to come together. Add more water if needed.

Take out of the processor and knead the dough for a minute or two on a lightly floured surface until the pastry is smooth.

Shape it into a round ball and flatten slightly into a disc shape. Wrap in plastic wrap and place in the fridge for 30 minutes.

Roll out the dough on a lightly floured surface until around 3mm (1/8 in) thick.

Place into the quiche dish. Fill the case with a layer of foil, then some baking beads or rice.

Bake for 10 minutes. Remove from oven and remove the foil and beads.

Reduce oven to 180°C (350°F, Gas Mark 4).

Heat the oil in a small frying pan over medium-high heat. Add the leek and sauté for 5 minutes.

In a mixing bowl, combine the leek with the rest of the filling ingredients. Pour into the pastry case and bake for 35 minutes, or until the quiche is set and the pastry is golden brown.

Grilled Pumpkin Salad

SERVES 2

½ medium butternut pumpkin, peeled and cut into thick wedges

3 tbsps olive oil

1 tsp chilli flakes

Pinch of salt and freshly ground pepper

(250g, 9oz) cherry tomatoes

¼ cup (30g, 1oz) pepitas (pumpkin seeds)

2 small complete heads of garlic, sliced in half crosswise

200g (7oz) rocket leaves, washed and dried

1 lemon, cut into wedges

Toss pumpkin together with 1 tablespoon of the olive oil, chilli flakes and salt and pepper, ensuring wedges are thoroughly coated. Remove pumpkin from the bowl, add tomatoes and toss with 2 teaspoons of olive oil. Drizzle the remaining oil over the cut halves of the heads of garlic. Heat a large grill plate or barbecue grill to medium-high heat. Place pumpkin wedges on the grill, along with the garlic halves, cut side up, and grill for 10 minutes. Add the tomatoes, flip the pumpkin and garlic over and grill for a further 10 minutes, turning the tomatoes frequently until the pumpkin is softened. Gently toss the vegetables and garlic together with rocket and pepitas, and serve with a lemon wedge on the side.

Chicken & Leek Tartlets

SERVES 6

6 pastry shells - pre-bought or see page 88 for pastry recipe

2 tbsps butter

3–4 leeks, chopped, white part only

½ small red capsicum, finely chopped

Pinch of salt

200g chicken fillet, sliced in half lengthways

1 cup (250ml, 8fl oz) thickened cream

2 eggs, beaten

¼ tsp pepper

½ cup (60g, 2oz) Swiss cheese, grated

2 tbsps chopped chives, to garnish

Melt 1 tablespoon of butter in a large frying pan over medium heat. Add leek, capsicum and salt and fry for 2 minutes, until leeks have softened. Remove from pan and set aside. Heat the rest of the butter then add the chicken and fry for 4 minutes on either side. Remove from the pan and shred into small pieces. Combine cream, eggs, chicken, leeks, capsicum and pepper in a medium bowl. Pour mixture into crust. Sprinkle cheese on top. Place in the oven and bake for 30 minutes, until filling is set and cheese is golden. Cool on a wire rack. Serve garnished with chopped chives

MIXED LEAVES

It might change your view on 'mixed leaves' if you knew that in days gone by the mixing of rocket (considered an aphrodisiac) and lettuce (considered calming) was a prudent measure to offset the stimulating effect of rocket! Stimulation aside, rocket is an excellent source of vitamins, minerals and other nutrients.

Chicken and Noodle Miso Soup with Egg

A PROTEIN-PACKED BOWL OF DELICIOUSNESS THAT ALLOWS YOU TO SHOWCASE YOUR JAPANESE CULINARY SKILLS WITH CONFIDENCE

SERVES 2

100g (3½ oz) noodles

1 tsp yellow or red miso

3 cups (750ml, 1 pt 9fl oz) water

2 tsps soy sauce

2 thin slices ginger, peeled and cut into matchsticks

1 clove garlic, thinly sliced

300g (10oz) chicken thighs, skin removed, cut into large pieces

2 spring onions, thinly sliced, plus extra for garnish

1 tsp ponzu sauce

2 eggs, room temperature

1 medium green chilli, seeded and sliced

1 tsp chilli flakes, to garnish

Cook the noodles according to the instructions on the packet. Drain. If using buckwheat noodles, rinse with cold water to remove excess starch.

Meanwhile, in a small bowl, whisk together the miso and ½ cup water.

Place the eggs in a small saucepan of cold water. Bring to a gentle simmer, gently stirring frequently. Simmer for 5 minutes, then remove and run briefly under cold water. Let cool.

In a medium-size saucepan, bring the remaining 2½ cups water, soy sauce, ginger and garlic to a boil. Reduce the heat and simmer for 10 minutes.

Add the chicken pieces and half the spring onions, and simmer for 2–3 minutes. Gently stir in the miso and ponzu sauce.

Peel the eggs and slice in half, lengthways.

Divide the noodles into two serving bowls. Equally portion out the chicken and onions over the noodles. Pour the soup liquid over. Place the egg halves, cut side up, in the soup as well.

Garnish with the remaining spring onions, plus green chilli and chilli flakes.

GOAT'S CHEESE

Goat's cheese is white, salty, smooth and creamy and perfect for spreading, dolloping or cooking with. It is lighter in texture than cow's milk cheese, lower in fat and contains less lactose, so is easier to digest. It's also richer in all the goody-goody nutrients, including vitamin A, vitamin B, calcium, iron, magnesium and potassium.

Called 'chevre' in French, goat's cheese sometimes comes encased in an edible rind that preserves its inner cream. Usually, though, it comes in a neat, round log that can be spread like soft butter onto a piece of rye toast, or scooped out in chunks for a classic goat's cheese and beetroot salad. A log of goat's cheese in the fridge means lunch or a late-night snack is always at hand — smooth it into omelettes or smear it on slices of avocado and barely a cracker is needed.

GOAT'S CHEESE PLATTER

Consider a goat's cheese platter with a range of cheeses made from these cute furry animals.

BRIE: Goat's milk can be used to make a version of Brie that is gooey and tangy and lighter on the waistline than the traditional Brie. A slice is divine on its own or layer it with tomatoes and fresh basil leaves for a sandwich without the bread.

CHEDDAR: Goat's cheese cheddar is light, sharp and tangy, and the colour of a mandarin.

HUMBOLDT FOG: Fluffy and velvety, Humboldt Fog is originally made in the US. It often has a stripe of blue through it for a smoky, savoury touch. Smear a slice with raw honey for a salty, sweet thrill.

TWO GOAT'S CHEESE CLASSICS

MARINATED GOAT'S CHEESE: Goat's cheese is beautiful paired with oils and seasonings that enhance the distinct goaty tang. Pour good olive oil over a log of cheese, add peppercorns and sprigs of rosemary or thyme and let it all marinate for a few hours or days in a sealed jar. Or try this with combinations of garlic, lemon rind, red chilli and herbs like parsley or chives. Scoop at it with fresh red capsicum or carrots.

GOAT'S CHEESE AND CARAMELIZED ONIONS: This is a beloved combination: the sweetness of the gooey, softened onions enhances the smooth, salty cheese. Fill an omelette and serve with a side of brown rice for a hearty meal. Scoop it into puff pastry with beaten eggs and bake for a savoury sweet tart. Or smear goat's cheese onto a portobello mushroom, top it with caramelized onions and garnish with fresh parsley for a high-energy vegetarian burger.

Summer Fruits and Goat's Cheese Salad with Lime Vinaigrette

A GORGEOUS COMBINATION OF SWEET, SALTY AND CITRUSY INGREDIENTS COMBINE IN THIS FANTASTIC LUNCH SALAD

SERVES 2-4

200g (7oz) fresh baby spinach leaves, rinsed

1 cup (200g, 7oz) strawberries, hulled and halved

2 yellow nectarines, sliced

½ cup (65g, 2oz) red seedless grapes, halved

1 cup (100g, 3½ oz) blueberries

1 small red onion, thinly sliced

200g (7oz) goat's cheese, crumbled

½ cup (60g, 2oz) walnuts, halved

LIME VINAIGRETTE

2 tbsps lime juice

½ tsp honey

¼ tsp cayenne pepper

½ tsp chilli powder

¼ cup (60ml, 2fl oz) extra virgin olive oil

Heat a small frying pan over medium-high heat and dry-fry the walnut halves for 5 minutes or until they begin to brown. Remove immediately from the pan and set aside.

In a large bowl add the fresh spinach. Top spinach with the fruit, red onion, walnuts and goat's cheese.

To make the vinaigrette, in a small bowl mix together lime juice, honey, cayenne pepper and chilli and then slowly drizzle in the olive oil, whisking until emulsified. Season to taste.

Pour dressing over salad and toss to combine.

Peach and Three Cheese Pizza

GOAT'S CHEESE ADDS AN EARTHY, SALTY FLAVOUR TO THIS
OTHERWISE SWEET AND CRUNCHY PIZZA

SERVES 2

BASE

2 cups (250g, 8oz)
baker's (or plain) flour

7g (¼ oz) sachet dry
active yeast

1 tsp salt

¾ cup (185ml, 6fl oz)
warm water

1 tbsp olive oil, plus
extra to grease

TOPPING

½ cup (60g, 2oz)
mozzarella cheese,
grated

100g (3½ oz) goat's
cheese Camembert, cut
into thin wedges

100g (3½ oz) goat's
cheese, crumbled

1 small red onion, sliced

1 peach, thinly sliced

1 tsp rosemary leaves,
chopped

1 tbsp honey (optional)

Extra rosemary leaves,
to garnish

To make the base, sift flour into a large mixing bowl. Stir in yeast and salt. Make a well in the centre and pour in water and oil. Bring the dough together with your hands, then turn out onto a lightly floured surface. Clean the bowl for reuse.

Knead for 5 minutes by hand (or in an electric mixer with a dough hook) until the dough is smooth.

Lightly grease the cleaned bowl with a little oil, then add dough and cover with a tea towel or plastic wrap. Set aside in a warm place to prove for 1 hour, until doubled in size.

Preheat oven to 240°C (465°F, Gas Mark 9). Lightly flour two baking trays.

Knock back the dough by punching it to remove air, and divide into two balls. Roll dough out on a lightly floured surface to create two very thin, 25cm (10in) diameter bases. Transfer to prepared baking sheets.

Drizzle olive oil on the pizza base. Scatter with grated mozzarella cheese and layer over the Camembert wedges, goat's cheese, onion, peach slices and rosemary leaves. Drizzle the honey over the top. Place in the oven and and bake for 10 minutes until cheese has melted and the pizza bases are crisp and golden around the edges.

Drizzle the pizzas with a little more olive oil, garnish with rosemary leaves then serve immediately.

Goat's Cheese Salad

SERVES 2-4

100g (3½ oz) goat's cheese, crumbled

200g (7oz) baby rocket leaves, washed and dried

18 pitted morello cherries, reserve 2 tbsps cherry liquid

2 tbsps butter

¼ cup (30g, 1oz) pistachios, finely chopped

¼ cup (30g, 1oz) fresh breadcrumbs

1 tbsp thyme leaves, chopped

1 tbsp sherry vinegar

1 tsp balsamic vinegar

Salt and freshly ground pepper

3 tbsps flaxseed oil

Heat the butter in a small frying pan over medium-heat. Fry pistachios, breadcrumbs and thyme, stirring constantly for 5 minutes, until toasted and crunchy. Set aside.

Combine the rocket, cherries and goat's cheese in a large bowl.

Whisk together the cherry liquid, vinegars, a couple of grinds of salt and pepper and the flaxseed oil. Toss the dressing and pistachio breadcrumb mix through the salad before serving.

Spinach & Ricotta Rolls

SERVES 4

500g (1lb 2oz) fresh ricotta

80g (3oz) Romano cheese, grated

200g (7oz) baby spinach leaves, roughly chopped

2 eggs, lightly beaten

Pinch of nutmeg

1 tsp salt

¼ tsp freshly ground black pepper

4 sheets puff pastry

2 tbsps sesame seeds

Egg wash (1 egg, lightly beaten with 1 tbsp water)

Preheat oven to 200°C (400°F, Gas Mark 6). Line two large flat baking trays with baking paper. Place the ricotta, cheese, baby spinach leaves, eggs, nutmeg and salt and pepper into a large bowl and stir until all of the ingredients have combined. Place pastry sheets on a flat working surface and cut each in half. Place equal portions of the ricotta mix along each half, leaving a gap from one edge. Lightly brush the long edges with the egg wash. Roll pastry over the ricotta mix. Place each roll, seam side down, on the baking trays. Brush the top of each roll with the rest of the egg wash and sprinkle with the sesame seeds. Cut each roll into quarters and bake in the oven for 30 minutes, or until golden brown.

RICOTTA

Ricotta is a very creamy, yet very light white cheese and can be made at home using full fat milk, preferably with the cream left on the top. It is high in protein and has just the right amount of fat to fill up the belly and stave off cravings. Use ricotta in salads with citrusy fruits and veggies like beetroots, peaches or tomatoes. It is an excellent texture for lasagne. Ricotta can also transform a pancake into a savoury dish and be used for baking vegetable breads and cakes.

Ricotta Pancakes and Strawberries

RICOTTA PROVIDES SUBSTANCE AND PROTEIN IN THESE BRUNCH
PANCAKES. HONEY'S AN OPTIONAL EXTRA!

SERVES 8-10

1 cup (225g, 8oz) fresh
ricotta cheese

1 cup (125g, 4oz) plain
flour

½ tsp baking powder

¼ tsp sea salt

¼ tsp cinnamon

2 large eggs, separated

1½ tsps maple syrup

¾ cup (185ml, 6fl oz)
soy milk

Butter, for cooking

1 cup (200g, 7oz) fresh
strawberries

¼ cup (90g, 3oz) honey
(optional)

Sift together the flour, baking powder, salt and cinnamon in a
small bowl.

In a large mixing bowl, mix together the ricotta, egg yolks, maple
syrup and milk.

Pour the dry ingredients into the ricotta mix and stir together
until thoroughly combined.

Whisk together the egg whites until stiff peaks form. Gently fold
them into the ricotta mix using a slotted spoon.

Melt the butter in a large frying pan over medium heat until it
starts to foam.

Pour ¼ cup amounts of the batter into the frying pan and fry
for 3 minutes, until bubbles start to form on the surface of the
pancakes.

Flip over and fry for another 3 minutes until golden brown.

Serve the pancakes immediately with strawberries and honey (if
using) drizzled over.

Family Dinners

BROWN IS BETTER

It can be a bit of a shift for the taste buds: white rice, white pasta and white flour are softer and sweeter than the brown versions. And for most, that's simply what we are used to. So why change?

Brown rice, whole-wheat flour and whole-wheat pasta are unrefined (or less refined), meaning they contain more nutrients from the plants they originally come from. A side bowl of brown rice, for example, contains about 10% of the daily requirement of vitamins and minerals essential for a healthy heart, muscles and immune system. But it's the fibre content of 'brown' that is the big winner. The bran layers of the original wheat plant are intact, and that's where the fibre is. Wheat is a carbohydrate, which is good for you only when it's accompanied by protein and fibre. Fibre allows the body to process the carbohydrates slowly, converting them into sustainable energy.

It's not all science: where white means light and sweet, brown often means nutty, buttery and savoury. White rice tastes like white sugar; brown rice like maple syrup. It's a shift for the taste buds, yes, but once made, it is rarely regretted.

WHOLE-WHEAT AND WHOLE-GRAIN PASTA

One cup of whole-wheat spaghetti contains about 23% of the recommended daily fibre compared with white pasta's 9%. Whole wheat also has 16% of the necessary protein and doses of B vitamins, iron and antioxidant properties.

There are also pastas made from all sorts of grains: buckwheat and quinoa are popular, and some blend whole-grain flour with legumes and flax, which give big-time boosts of protein and omega-3 good fats. Whole-grain pastas are trickier to cook as they are more complex in structure. The goal is to avoid mush and the taste test is the best method. If a packet says boil for 12 minutes, then take a bite around the 8-minute mark. If there's a ring of white inside, keep cooking. The minute this disappears, the pasta is as close to the al dente crunch as it gets.

RYE NOT?

Try rye bread, which is gluten-free and has more protein and fibre than most store-bought breads. Rye has a rich taste and is an excellent choice for bread puddings or croutons, or try rye flour for baking.

BROWN RICE FLOUR

For battered fish and tempura vegetables, try brown rice flour, which is gluten-free and rich in protein. Brown rice flour is excellent for thickening sauces and baking into cakes and biscuits.

Baked Salmon with Vegetables

THIS TASTY DINNER IS SO VERSATILE, AS YOU CAN SWAP
THE VEGGIES ACCORDING TO THE SEASON

SERVES 4

4 x 200g (7oz) salmon
fillets, skin on

3 cloves garlic, minced

¼ cup (60ml, 2fl oz)
coconut oil

2 tsps sea salt

2 tsps green
peppercorns in brine,
drained

Freshly ground black
pepper

500g (1lb 2oz) Brussels
sprouts, ends trimmed

2 cups (200g, 7oz)
broccoli florets

2 tsps lemon zest

250g (9oz) cherry
tomatoes

6 small rosemary sprigs

1 lemon, halved and
sliced

¾ cup (185ml, 6fl oz)
white wine (such as
sauvignon blanc)

Preheat oven to 230°C (450°F, Gas Mark 8).

In a small bowl, combine the garlic, 2 tablespoons coconut oil,
salt, peppercorns and a couple of good grinds of pepper. Brush
over the salmon fillets and set them aside.

Cut a cross into the bottom of each Brussels sprout with a sharp
knife (this will help them cook evenly) then bring a large pot of
salted water to the boil. Add the Brussels sprouts and boil for
4 minutes. Add the broccoli and boil for a further 2 minutes.
Drain the vegetables.

Gently toss the broccoli and sprouts with the rest of the coconut
oil and the lemon zest in a large bowl.

Scatter the broccoli, sprouts and tomatoes in the bottom of a
large, high-sided roasting pan. Bake in the oven for 10 minutes.

Nestle the salmon fillets in the vegetables, scatter the rosemary
sprigs over the top with a couple of the lemon slices. Splash the
wine over the top.

Bake for a further 10 minutes or until the salmon is cooked
through.

Let sit for 5 minutes before serving.

Moussaka

THIS HEARTY OPTION DELIVERS SUBSTANCE, FLAVOUR AND NUTRITIONAL PUNCH TO YOUR FAMILY'S DINNER TABLE

SERVES 6

3 eggplants, thinly sliced lengthways

Olive oil, for brushing, plus ½ tbsp, for frying

2 onions, finely chopped

2 cloves garlic, finely chopped

765g (1½ lb) lamb mince

½ tsp nutmeg (optional)

2 tbsps tomato paste

1 x 400g (14oz) can chopped tomatoes

1 bay leaf

3 tbsps fresh oregano, chopped (or 2 tsp dried)

1 stick cinnamon (optional)

2 large potatoes, peeled and very thinly sliced lengthways

½ cup (50g, 2oz) Parmesan cheese, grated

1 tbsp fresh parsley, chopped

SAUCE

2 tbsps butter

2 tbsps plain flour

2 cups (500ml, 1pt) milk

½ cup (60g, 2oz) Cheddar cheese, grated

Preheat the oven to 180°C (350°F, Gas Mark 4) and prepare a large baking tray with baking paper.

Place eggplant slices on baking tray and lightly brush with oil. Place in the oven and bake for 10 minutes.

Meanwhile, heat oil in a frying pan over medium-high heat. Add onions and garlic and sauté for 5 minutes until soft. Add lamb mince and nutmeg and cook for a further 4–5 minutes, stirring to ensure even browning. Add tomato paste, canned tomatoes, bay leaf, oregano and cinnamon (if using), and season with salt and pepper. Stir to combine and simmer over a low heat.

To make the sauce, heat the butter in a saucepan over low heat. Add flour and mix until a smooth, thick paste forms. Gradually add the milk and gently bring to the boil, stirring constantly. Add the Cheddar cheese and stir through until melted.

Remove cinnamon stick and bay leaf from mince mixture and discard.

Assemble the moussaka in a deep-sided ovenproof dish. Layer one-third of the eggplant to cover the base. Top with half of the potatoes and half the mince, then a third of the cheese sauce. Add another layer of eggplant, potatoes, mince and a third of the cheese sauce. Add a final layer of the eggplant and cheese sauce, and finish with the grated Parmesan cheese.

Place in the oven and bake for 30 minutes until the potatoes are fully cooked and cheese is golden.

Serve garnished with fresh parsley.

Brown Rice Risotto

SERVES 4

5 cups (1.25L, 2pt 10fl oz) chicken (or vegetable) stock, warmed

3 tbsps butter

1 onion, finely chopped

400g (14oz) button mushrooms, thinly sliced

1 tbsp thyme leaves (or dried thyme)

2 cups (310g, 8oz) Arborio rice

½ cup (125ml, 4fl oz) dry white wine

½ cup (50g, 2oz) Parmesan cheese, grated

Salt and black pepper, to season

Parmesan shavings, to serve

2 tbsps fresh parsley leaves, chopped

Melt the butter in a deep-sided saucepan over medium-high heat. Add onion and cook, stirring, for 3–4 minutes until soft. Add mushrooms and thyme and sauté for 5 minutes. Add the rice and stir to combine. Pour in wine and simmer, uncovered, until liquid has reduced. Reduce heat to low and stir in half a cup of stock at a time until the liquid has fully absorbed. The risotto is done when the rice is tender but still firm to bite. Stir in the Parmesan cheese and season to taste with salt and pepper. Garnish with shaved Parmesan and parsley.

Slow-Roasted Beef

SERVES 6

1.2kg (2½ lb) beef for roasting (preferably blade), at room temperature

2 tbsps olive oil

1 tbsp Dijon mustard

1 tbsp soy sauce

1 tbsp maple syrup

1 tsp cayenne pepper

1 tsp balsamic vinegar

1 tsp sea salt

Freshly ground black pepper

Preheat oven to 150°C (290°F, Gas Mark 2). Combine oil, mustard, soy sauce, maple syrup, cayenne, vinegar, salt and a couple of good grinds of pepper together in a small bowl. Coat the roast with the mixture. Place the beef in a roasting tray and transfer to the oven. Place a small oven-proof bowl of water in the oven and ensure it is always full throughout the cooking period. Roast the beef in the oven for 4 hours, until falling apart and tender. Remove from oven, cover with foil and let it sit for 15 minutes before serving. Carve and serve hot.

HORSERADISH SAUCE

Horseradish is a root vegetable that is part of the broccoli family — and yet it tastes so different. It tastes pungent like radish and has a spicy, mustardy bite. The root is white and crunchy and high in fibre, vitamin C and minerals that are amazing for the immune system and for digestion. Horseradish often comes pickled in vinegar and it can be made into different sauces that pack flavour without a lick of fat or sugar. A simple sauce recipe mixes horseradish with sour cream, chives and lemon juice.

Pork Meatballs with Garlic Yoghurt Dip

AN EASY, TASTY DINNER THAT BRINGS TOGETHER A FUSION OF ASIAN AND EUROPEAN FLAVOURS

SERVES 6

500g (1lb 2oz) pork mince

1 tbsp ginger, minced

5 cloves garlic, minced

¼ cup (60ml, 2fl oz) soy sauce

3 tsps sesame oil

1 cup (125g, 4oz) whole-wheat breadcrumbs

3 tbsps coriander, finely chopped

1 tsp ground fennel seeds

2 eggs, beaten

GARLIC YOGHURT DIP

1 clove garlic, minced

1 tsp lemon rind, finely grated

1½ cups (375g, 13oz) Greek yoghurt

Salt and pepper, to season

Preheat the oven to 200°C (400°F, Gas Mark 6) and line a baking tray with baking paper.

Place mince, ginger, garlic, soy sauce, sesame oil, breadcrumbs, coriander, fennel and eggs in a large mixing bowl. Stir to combine initially and then bring together with hands until thoroughly combined.

Shape into bite-sized meatballs. Place meatballs on the baking tray.

Transfer to the oven and bake for 10 minutes or until cooked through.

To make the dip, place garlic, lemon rind and yoghurt in a bowl. Season with salt and pepper. Stir to combine.

Baked Blue-Eye with Anchovy Crust

SALTY AND EARTHY FLAVOURS COMBINE IN THIS MEDITERRANEAN-STYLE FISH DINNER

SERVES 6

6 x 200g (7oz) fillets blue-eye, deboned, skin removed

¹⁄₃ cup (80ml, 3fl oz) olive oil

3 cloves garlic, minced

2 red onions, chopped

6 thick slices stale whole-wheat bread, crusts removed

6 marinated anchovy fillets, drained and chopped

1 cup (125g, 4oz) flaked almonds

2 tsps cayenne pepper

100g (3½ oz) butter, cut into cubes and chilled

2 tbsps fresh basil leaves, chopped

½ cup (20g, ¾ oz) fresh parsley leaves, roughly chopped

1 lemon, cut into wedges, to serve

Salt and pepper, to season

Preheat oven to 200°C (400°F, Gas Mark 6).

Heat 2 tablespoons of oil in a large frying pan over medium-low heat. Add the onion and garlic and sauté for 20 minutes, until the onion is translucent.

Lay the bread slices in a shallow baking tray, season with salt and pepper and drizzle with 2 tablespoons olive oil.

Place the blue-eye fillets on top of the bread, season and place in the oven for 8 minutes.

Place the anchovy, half the almonds, cayenne pepper, butter, basil and parsley in the food processer and pulse a couple of times until it's a rough crumb mixture.

Remove from the processor and mix together with the onion and the rest of the almonds.

Spread the crumbs over the fillets and place back in the oven.

Bake for 15 minutes, until the mixture starts to crisp.

Serve warm with lemon wedges on the side.

ASPARAGUS

The gorgeous green spears of asparagus are at their peak in springtime. Asparagus is full of flavour and fibre and very low in calories. It's also a vitamin superstar — crunch four spears and get dosed up on vitamins C, K, B6 and E as well as potassium for blood pressure. It's a metabolism booster, which apparently involves an enzyme that helps the liver metabolize alcohol — helpful for hangovers! Roast asparagus spears with Brazil nuts and butter, stir-fry them with chives and bacon, or steam them and douse in lemon, Parmesan cheese and pepper. Asparagus soup is also a comforting remedy.

Asparagus Cream Soup

SERVES 4–6

3 tbsps olive oil

6 shallots, peeled and sliced

3 cloves garlic, minced

2 large bunches asparagus, woody ends trimmed

6 cups (1.5L, 3pt 3fl oz) vegetable stock

½ tsp sea salt

Freshly ground black pepper

2 tbsps lemon juice

¼ cup (25g, 1oz) Parmesan cheese, grated

¼ cup (60g, 2oz) Greek yoghurt

Cut off the tips of the asparagus spears and reserve. Roughly chop remaining parts of the stems. Heat oil in a saucepan over medium heat. Add shallots and garlic and fry for 10 minutes, then add chopped asparagus, stock, salt and pepper. Bring to the boil, then reduce the heat to low and simmer, covered, for 30 minutes. Transfer to blender, stir in lemon juice, yoghurt and Parmesan, process until smooth. Bring saucepan of salted water to the boil and cook asparagus tips for 2 minutes. Drain and set aside. Gently reheat the soup until almost simmering. Season to taste and serve garnished with the asparagus tips.

Asparagus with Pine Nuts

SERVES 2

1 tbsp olive oil

1 bunch asparagus, woody ends trimmed

¼ cup (35g, 1¼ oz) pine nuts

¼ cup (40g, 1½ oz) dried cranberries (optional)

2 wedges lemon

Heat a small frying pan over medium-high heat and dry-fry the pine nuts for 3 minutes or until they begin to brown. Remove immediately from the pan and set aside.

Heat oil in a large frying pan over medium-high heat. Add asparagus and sauté for 3–4 minutes, until just tender.

Remove the asparagus with a slotted spoon and squeeze the lemon wedges over them.

Serve the asparagus warm with pine nuts and cranberries (if using).

Hot Japanese Ramen

BRING THIS CLASSIC JAPANESE SOUP INTO YOUR OWN KITCHEN WITH EASE

SERVES 2

2 tsps sesame or vegetable oil

2 cloves garlic, thinly sliced

2 tsps fresh ginger, finely sliced

3 tbsps tamari

2 tbsps mirin

4 cups (1L, 2pt) rich chicken stock

½ tsp chilli powder

1 tsp salt

180g (6oz) ramen noodles (dried or fresh)

100g (3½ oz) green beans

2 spring onions, cut into 3cm (1in) lengths

3 stems Chinese broccoli, cut into 3cm (1in) lengths

100g (3½ oz) straw mushrooms, ends trimmed

100g (3½ oz) shitake mushrooms, sliced

Salt and pepper, to season

Heat the oil in a large saucepan over medium heat, until shimmering. Add the garlic and ginger and cook until softened. Add the tamari and mirin, and stir to combine. Cook for another minute. Add the stock and chilli powder, cover, and bring to boil. Remove the lid and let simmer uncovered for 5 minutes, then add the mushrooms and vegetables. Simmer gently for another 10 minutes, and season with salt to taste.

Bring a medium saucepan of lightly salted water to the boil. Add the ramen noodles to the boiling water. Cook for 2–3 minutes, until soft, then drain.

Divide the noodles between two large soup bowls. Divide the greens and vegetables and place over the noodles, then pour the broth over the top.

Soba Noodle Stir-Fry with Beef and Vegetables

THIS DELICIOUS DINNER CONTAINS MORE TASTY VEGGIES THAN YOU CAN POKE A CHOPSTICK AT!

SERVES 4

400g (14oz) soba noodles

1 tsp sesame oil

2 tsps peanut oil

1kg (2lb) beef, cut into thin slices

3 cloves garlic, minced

Small piece ginger, peeled and cut into matchsticks

2 small red chillies, seeded and finely chopped

1 carrot, grated

1 red capsicum, sliced

1 yellow capsicum, sliced

1 cup (100g, 3½ oz) broccoli florets

1 bunch Chinese broccoli, cut into 4cm (1½ in) sections

200g (7oz) green beans, ends trimmed

½ cup (20g, ¾ oz) coriander leaves, roughly chopped

2 tbsps lime juice

¼ cup (60ml, 2fl oz) soy sauce

3 tbsps rice wine

3 tbsps honey

2 tbsps sesame seeds

Cook the noodles according to the directions on the packet. Drain and stir through the sesame oil to prevent them sticking together.

Heat a wok until very hot, then add the peanut oil. Stir-fry the beef, garlic, ginger and chillies for 3 minutes. Remove the beef from the wok and set aside.

Add the carrot, capsicum, broccoli, beans and coriander to the wok. Cook over high heat for 4 minutes, until softened.

Add the lime juice, soy sauce, rice wine and honey. Cook until the liquid has reduced by two-thirds.

Return the beef to the pan along with the sesame seeds. Add the noodles and toss to combine and heat through.

LIME

Fruit is nature's sugar. There are debates in the health-food world over the 'f' word — the fructose that's contained in all refined and sugary treats and is also naturally present in fruit. Pure fructose gives an energy shot that won't last until the next hour. It's the fibre and protein in fruit that balances out fructose and allows it to slowly convert into the bloodstream and digestive system. Nature made fruit to satisfy sweet cravings and to deliver good stuff at the same time. The general rule of thumb is: two servings a day for all the vitamins and nutrients we need, as well as the sweet fix. For the healthiest sugar fix, go for fruits like berries and kiwi fruit that have the highest fibre content. Or for a totally clear conscience, eat limes!

Limes are, in fact, the only fruit that have no fructose content. They are also tangy, fleshy little ovals of vitamin C, potassium and antioxidants that are heart-healthy. Limes deliver all of these wonderful health benefits and are also superstars in the kitchen, providing us with one of the easiest seasonings and flavours to cook with. Lime juice is amazing on its own — less tart than lemon — and is a perfect equalizer for salad dressings involving strong flavours like vinegar and Asian fish sauce.

A FEW EASY WAYS WITH LIME

AVOCADOS AND LIME: These two incredible fruits always make a healthy meal. Avocados can be smashed with lime juice and maybe salt and pepper and there's a super-simple guacamole. Or simply slice avocados, douse in lime juice and layer these over a grilled tuna steak. Sprinkle on some parsley for extra crunch and fibre.

ASIAN SALAD: Lime juice is essential for Asian-inspired salads combining chicken or pork with tropical fruits like mango or pawpaw. Toss in spring onions, chilli and peanuts for the real deal. Lime juice is also a handy seasoning to have around for Asian noodle dishes and stir-fries.

PRESERVED LIMES: Like lemons, limes just need salt, their own juice and time to preserve into fleshier, saltier versions of themselves to use in cooking.

CUCUMBER, BASIL AND LIME JUICE: A not-naughty mojito, this juice is super-refreshing and equally sweet as savoury. The cucumber, basil and ice mellow out the tartness of the lime juice. A juicer is great to have, or use a blender. Blend or juice a handful of basil leaves, a cucumber, half a lime and an apple.

Lime and Pepper Grilled Chicken Breast

THE CONTRASTING FLAVOURS OF LIME, SOY AND PALM SUGAR
MAKE FOR A TANGY YET SWEETLY DELICIOUS DINNER OPTION

SERVES 4

½ cup (125ml, 4fl oz) fresh lime juice

2 cloves garlic, minced

3 tbsps palm sugar (or brown sugar)

2 tbsps freshly ground black pepper

1 tbsp coconut oil

2 tbsps soy sauce

1 tsp sea salt

4 small chicken breasts, skin removed

Spring onions, sliced, to garnish

Fresh lime wedges, to serve

Whisk together the lime juice, garlic, sugar, pepper, oil, soy sauce, salt, and ¼ cup water in a small bowl until the sugar is dissolved. Set aside.

Flatten the chicken fillets by placing them in freezer bags and pounding with a tenderizer or a rolling pin. You want to get them to 1cm (½ in) thick if you can.

Coat the breasts in the marinade and place in the fridge for at least 2 hours.

Heat a grill pan or barbecue grill to high heat.

Grill the chicken breasts for 4 minutes on either side until cooked through.

Serve hot with spring onions sprinkled over as garnish.

Pork Larb Lettuce Wraps

THESE FRESH, CRUNCHY WRAPS ARE FUN TO CREATE AND CAN BE AN APPETIZER OR THE MAIN EVENT

SERVES 2

FILLING

1 tbsp coconut oil

4 cloves garlic, minced

1 tsp palm sugar (or brown sugar)

1 tsp chilli powder

300g (10oz) pork mince

1 tsp fish sauce

½ tsp tamari

Salt and freshly ground black pepper

TO SERVE

1 head butter or iceberg lettuce

¼ cup (10g, ¼ oz) coriander leaves

1 Lebanese cucumber, chopped

1 red onion, finely chopped

1 lime, cut into quarters

Heat the oil in a medium frying pan over medium-high heat. Add the garlic and sauté for 1 minute. Add the sugar, chilli powder and pork and fry for 5 minutes, breaking up the pork, until it is cooked through.

Stir in the fish sauce, tamari and a couple of good grinds of salt and pepper to taste.

Transfer the pork mixture to a serving bowl and set aside.

To assemble, take a whole lettuce leaf and place a small amount of the pork mixture inside it. Top with small amounts of coriander, cucumber and onion. Squeeze over a small amount of lime juice.

Mediterranean Chicken and Vegetable Soup

WHOLESOME AND SOULSOME, THIS SOUP IS A SPECIAL MIDWEEK PICK-ME-UP

SERVES 6

1 tbsp sesame seeds

4 cups (1L, 2pt) chicken stock

¼ cup (60ml, 2fl oz) olive oil

1 tbsp raw sugar

1 tsp sea salt

Freshly ground black pepper

2 large chicken breasts, cut into small cubes

3 tomatoes, chopped

3 zucchinis, finely julienned

1 cup (175g, 6oz) broad beans, shelled

1 carrot, grated

1 tbsp chilli flakes

¼ cup (10g, ¼ oz) parsley leaves, roughly chopped

½ cup semi-dried tomatoes, finely chopped

1 tsp chilli powder

2 tbsps oregano leaves, chopped

Heat a small frying pan over medium-high heat and dry-fry the sesame seeds for 2 minutes or until they begin to brown. Remove immediately from the pan and set aside.

In a large heavy pot, bring the stock to the boil. Add 1 tablespoon of oil, sugar and salt and a couple of good grinds of pepper.

Add the chicken, bring to the boil and cook for 6 minutes, then reduce the heat to low and simmer until the chicken is cooked through.

Add the tomatoes, zucchini, beans, carrot, chilli flakes and half the parsley. Bring to the boil again, then reduce and cook for 2 minutes.

Heat the rest of the oil in a small saucepan over medium heat. Fry the semi-dried tomatoes and chilli powder together for 2 minutes. Remove from heat.

Serve the soup topped with the remaining parsley, oregano, sesame seeds and a small amount of the semi-dried tomato mix.

Cornflake-Crusted Chicken

SERVES 4

4 medium chicken breasts, skin removed

3 cups (90g, 3oz) cornflakes, crushed

2 tbsps coconut oil

1 tsp celery salt

¼ cup (30g, 1oz) plain flour

½ tsp sea salt

Freshly ground pepper

1 large egg, lightly beaten

1 tsp water

Preheat oven to 190°C (375°F, Gas Mark 5). Line a large flat baking tray with baking paper. Mix together the cornflakes, coconut oil and celery salt and place in shallow dish. Mix together the flour, salt and a good couple of grinds of pepper and place in a shallow bowl. Whisk together the egg and water in a bowl. Pat dry the breasts then coat in the flour, shaking off any excess. Dip each breast into the egg wash then in the cornflake mix to coat. The mix will be slightly moist so you may have to press it onto the fillets. Place the fillets on the baking tray and press in any extra flakes. Bake for 35 minutes, or until crispy and golden brown.

Chicken with Tarragon Sauce

SERVES 4

4 tbsps butter

4 spring onions, chopped

2 cloves garlic, crushed

4 medium chicken breasts, skin removed

1 tbsp flour

2 tsps Dijon mustard

1 cup (250ml, 8fl oz) dry white wine

1 tbsp lemon juice

2 tsps fresh tarragon, chopped

½ cup (125ml, 4fl oz) thickened cream

1 tbsp tarragon leaves, to garnish

Heat 2 tablespoons of the butter in a large frying pan over medium-high heat. Add onion and garlic and fry for 3 minutes. Add chicken and fry for 4 minutes either side, then remove from pan and sit in a warm place. Add the rest of the butter and melt over medium heat. Stir in flour and cook for 1 minute, add the mustard and stir through. Slowly add the wine, stirring constantly. Add the lemon juice, tarragon, cream and season with salt and pepper. Heat until just simmering, then serve poured over the chicken breasts and garnished with tarragon leaves.

TARRAGON

Peppery with the sweetness of vanilla, this pungent, aromatic herb is an excellent seasoning for chicken, pork or rice. It's lovely in any dish involving whipped cream or light, white cheeses, and amazing in scrambled eggs. This all-rounder herb contains compounds shown to naturally lower blood sugar levels, which is why it's a great seasoning for starchy foods like potatoes — roast, bake or mash them with tarragon and pepper and indulge while getting the bloodstream pumping with antioxidants and minerals that are good for the heart.

Roast Chicken with Chickpea Stuffing

YOU GOTTA LOVE THIS HIGH-PROTEIN, LOW-GI TWIST ON TRADITIONAL STUFFING FOR THE SUNDAY ROAST

SERVES 4–6

1 large chicken

1 bunch sage leaves, roughly chopped

2 tbsps parsley leaves, chopped

2 cloves garlic, minced

200g (7oz) butter, at room temperature

1/3 cup (80ml, 3fl oz) olive oil

3 tbsps salt flakes

Sea salt and freshly ground black pepper

STUFFING

2 tbsps olive oil, plus extra for chickpeas

1 onion, chopped

1 tsp ground cumin

1 tsp ground oregano

2 red chillies, sliced

1 lemon, zested

1 x 400g (14oz) can chickpeas, drained and rinsed

¼ cup (10g, ¼ oz) oregano leaves, roughly chopped

1 large lemon, halved

2 spring onions, sliced, for garnish

Preheat oven to 200°C (400°F, Gas Mark 6).

Season the inside of the chicken.

Mix the sage, parsley, garlic and butter together in a small bowl.

Gently slide your fingers up under the chicken skin and push the herb butter inside the gaps you've just made.

To make the stuffing, heat the oil in a large frying pan over medium-high heat. Add the onion and sauté for 5 minutes, until the onion is translucent.

Add the cumin, ground oregano, chillies and lemon zest. Fry for 2 more minutes. Mix together with the chickpeas, oregano leaves and a slug of olive oil.

Spoon the stuffing into the chicken cavity and block the cavity with half a lemon.

Season the chicken with the salt flakes and olive oil, rubbing both heavily into the skin.

Roast in the oven for 50 minutes until golden brown.

To serve, remove the stuffing and place in a serving bowl alongside the chicken.

Garnish the stuffing with spring onion slices.

BARLEY

It's nutty, fluffy, a bit crunchy, and as cosy to eat as pasta when you get used to it, but barley is a grain that is somehow overshadowed by 'super' grains such as quinoa and buckwheat. Yet barley deserves the super status for its combination dietary fibres alone, as these give it a low position on the GI index. It both balances and lowers blood sugar and insulin levels, helping to combat type 2 diabetes and heart disease. In addition, barley contains the rare antioxidant ferulic acid, which is good for the brain, and it also promotes good bacteria in the gut that cool down inflammation, the culprit behind many chronic diseases.

Most barley is referred to as 'pearl barley' — light and puffy, it looks like little pearls when boiled and steamed. Black barley is less refined and contains the most nutrients. Hulled barley has more nutritional oomph than unhulled, though it is a little trickier to soften for eating.

BARLEY CLASSICS

The health benefits make barley a grain to put on the menu. Where there is a liquidy broth, add barley for soup with a silky texture. Where there is usually rice or pasta, try barley. Where there is the word 'burger', try barley and vegetables to create high-energy burgers.

MUSHROOM BARLEY SOUP: Barley is a staple in soups in many different cuisines. Mushroom barley soup is a popular comfort food. In Armenia, barley soup with yoghurt and mint is a surprising summer dish that can definitely straddle the seasonal lines: simmer barley in chicken stock seasoned with a bay leaf. Whisk yoghurt with egg yolks, lemon zest and dried mint leaves. Combine it all for a light, creamy treat.

BARLEY RISOTTO: Sauté barley in a warm base of butter and onions. Add chicken stock and seasonings of parsley, dill or tarragon — or all three — and simmer for about 30 minutes until the barley is soft. Drain and cool. Stir in poached chicken strips and lightly fried cremini or shitake mushrooms, and serve with a garnish of chives and a spoon of plain yoghurt for a creamy stir.

BARLEY 'BURGERS': Mix cooked barley with chopped, grilled, hearty and bright vegetables such as eggplant, carrot, parsnip and capsicum. Throw them in a mixing bowl. Add blended chickpeas or cannellini beans that will be the paste that binds all these ingredients together into burgers, then bake until crisp. Add crushed cashews or pine nuts for extra protein and nutty crunch. Burger coma be gone!

Bean and Barley Porridge with Spinach

THIS COMFORTING BOWL OF PORRIDGE DELIVERS MANY NUTRITIONAL BENEFITS — AND FEEL-GOOD BENEFITS TOO

SERVES 4

1½ cups (275g, 9oz) barley

3 cups (750ml, 24fl oz) water

½ tsp salt

2 tbsps olive oil

1 large onion, chopped

2 cloves garlic, minced

400g (14oz) button mushrooms, sliced

1 large bunch of spinach, leaves torn

1 large tomato, chopped

1 tbsp lemon zest

1 tbsp basil leaves, chopped

1 x 400g (14oz) can cannellini beans, drained and rinsed

¼ cup (30g, 1oz) tasty cheese, grated

Salt and pepper, to taste

Place the barley, water and salt in a large saucepan over medium-high heat. Bring to the boil, then reduce heat to low and cover the pan. Simmer for 45 minutes, or until liquid is absorbed. Drain and set aside.

While the barley cooks, heat oil in a large frying pan over a medium heat.

Add onion and garlic and cook for 5 minutes.

Add mushrooms and cook for 5 minutes, until tender.

Add spinach and chopped tomato and a pinch of salt and cook for 1–2 minutes until spinach wilts.

Remove from heat and place into a large bowl. Add lemon zest, basil and beans and stir to combine.

Stir in the barley and mix ingredients together until just combined.

Serve warm. Season to taste with salt and pepper. Top with a small amount of tasty cheese for garnish.

Turkey Meatballs with Barley

A TURKEY TWIST ON THE CLASSIC MEATBALL THAT WILL FILL THE KIDS UP IN NO TIME

SERVES 2-4

450g (1lb) turkey mince

2 eggs, lightly beaten

¼ cup (50g, 2oz) pearl barley

1 cup (250ml, 8fl oz) vegetable stock

1 small onion, finely chopped

¼ cup (30g, 1oz) fresh breadcrumbs

1 tsp tamari

1 tsp olive oil

1 tsp cayenne pepper

1 tsp ground oregano

1 tsp salt

Freshly ground black pepper

3 tbsps olive oil

1 tbsp rosemary leaves, to garnish

Place the stock and barley in a small saucepan and bring to the boil. Reduce the heat to low and simmer, covered, for 40 minutes, until the barley is tender.

Drain the barley and place in a food processor. Pulse a couple of times to break up the barley into smaller pieces.

In a medium-sized mixing bowl mix together the turkey, eggs, barley, onion, breadcrumbs, tamari, oil, cayenne, oregano, salt and a couple of good grinds of black pepper. Mix with your hands until thoroughly combined.

Shape the mixture into small spoonfuls. The mixture should make about 16 small meatballs.

Heat the oil in a large, heavy frying pan over medium-high heat. Fry the meatballs for 8 minutes, turning frequently to brown all over.

Serve hot, garnished with fresh rosemary leaves.

Risotto with Pork Sausage and Vegetables

THIS WARMING COMFORT MEAL DELIVERS FLAVOUR, SUBSTANCE AND PLENTY OF GOOD NUTRIENTS

SERVES 6-8

4 tbsps olive oil

1 large onion, finely chopped

3 cloves garlic, crushed

600g (1lb 5oz) pork sausages

2 tsps chilli flakes

500g (1lb) button mushrooms, chopped

2 cups (310g, 8oz) Arborio rice

1 cup (250ml, 8fl oz) dry white wine (such as sauvignon blanc)

4½ cups (1.25L, 2pt 6fl oz) hot vegetable stock

3 carrots, chopped

1 yellow capsicum, chopped

1 red capsicum, chopped

1 small head of broccoli, broken into small florets

¹⁄₃ cup (35g, 1¼ oz) Parmesan cheese, grated

Salt and freshly ground pepper

¼ cup (10g, ¼ oz) fresh dill, chopped

Heat the oil in a large, high-sided frying pan over medium-high heat. Add the onion and garlic and sauté for 5 minutes, until the onion is translucent.

Add the sausages and fry for 5 minutes, until mostly cooked. Remove from the pan and carefully (so you don't burn yourself!) chop into small cubes.

Add the chilli and mushrooms and fry for 2 minutes until the mushrooms have softened. Add the Arborio rice and stir for 2 minutes until the rice grains are translucent.

Add the wine and stir until the liquid is absorbed. Then add the stock, a cup at a time, and stir until all the liquid is absorbed each time.

Straight after adding the fourth cup of stock, add the carrot, capsicums and broccoli. Continue stirring until all stock is absorbed.

Stir through the pork sausage and Parmesan cheese and heat through.

Serve garnished with fresh dill.

Snacks

IT'S A DATE

A lot of diets and recipes call for dried fruits in place of sugar. It might be a handful of dried apricots or cranberries for a snack in place of a chocolate biscuit, or the premier medjool dates in place of caramel in a toffee pudding or a chocolate mousse. Yet, there's mixed messaging on how healthy these delicious, sweet natural treats are.

THE LOW-DOWN ON DATES

Dates are a common go-to in low fat and low sugar recipes. The medjool variety are dark, golden brown, and look and taste like a blob of caramel picked straight from the tree. Their flesh is grainy and sugary; their skin is shiny and translucent. And the truth is, they are both healthy *and* contain a lot of sugar. Dates are high in fructose, and while their fibre content is also high for a fruit, it does not match the sugar content — dates contain 29mg of fructose, which makes them high on the GI index, meaning they will increase blood sugar levels. This isn't good for sugar cravings or for people at risk of diabetes.

That's the bad news over. Ultimately, that deliciously creamy and naturally sweet slice made with dates is infinitely healthier than a triple mud chocolate cake made in the traditional way. Dates are cholesterol-free and very low in fat. Plus they boast health benefits that white sugar will never be credited for. Dates are full of vitamin B, A and C. And the list keeps going: dates contain protein, iron, potassium, calcium and magnesium. They are good for the digestive system, balancing gut bacteria with some of the essential amino acids.

How to navigate these mixed blessings? Use dates and other dried fruit in place of sugar and know that there's a bunch of good stuff happening along with a bit of a naughty sugar rush. However, be moderate. It's possible to eat many more dried cranberries, sultanas and apricots than it is to polish off a whole bowl of fresh fruit. Treat dried fruits as fresh fruit is consumed: one apple or maybe two apricots in one sitting.

DATE TREATS

PUREED DATES: Pureed dates with a dollop of cream is a blissful quick snack.

DATE, COCONUT AND CACAO BALLS: Compact and full of energy and good fat. Soak dates for an hour to soften. Add to the blender with shredded coconut, cacao powder, chia seeds and almond meal. Mix until a moist paste. Roll into small balls — bite-sized portions — and roll around in extra shredded coconut. Eat fresh or refrigerate for days.

Passionfruit Chia Pudding

THIS BEAUTIFUL, CREAMY DESSERT IS NATURALLY SWEET AND
ALSO CONTAINS SUPER SEEDS AND ENERGY-BOOSTING NUTS

SERVES 2

CHIA

4 tbsps white chia
seeds

1½ cups (375ml, 13fl
oz) coconut milk

½ tsp vanilla extract

Pinch of sea salt

Pulp from 2 passionfruit

CASHEW CREAM

1 cup (125g, 4oz) raw
cashews

½ cup (125ml, 4fl oz)
filtered water, plus more
for soaking

1 tbsp maple syrup

½ tsp vanilla extract

Pinch of sea salt

TOPPING

1 mandarin, segmented,
skin and membrane
removed

¼ cup (25g, 1oz) fresh
blueberries

Mint leaves, to garnish

Place chia seeds, coconut milk, vanilla, passionfruit pulp and salt
into a bowl and cover with plastic wrap. Transfer to the fridge to
soak overnight.

To make the cashew cream, soak the cashews in a bowl of water
overnight.

Strain the cashews and place in a blender with the filtered water,
maple syrup, vanilla and salt and puree until smooth.

When ready to serve, divide the chia seed mixture between
2 serving glasses or bowls.

Spoon a layer of cashew cream over the chia mixture.

Top with mandarin segments and blueberries and garnish with
fresh mint leaves.

Summer Tart

THESE FRESH FLAVOURSOME TARTS ARE GREAT FOR QUICK SNACK AT HOME OR TO SHARE AT A PICNIC

SERVES 4

2 sheets puff pastry

200g (7oz) goat's cheese, crumbled

Pinch of nutmeg

½ cup (90g, 3oz) kalamata olives, pitted and roughly chopped

Salt and pepper to taste

⅓ cup (80ml, 3fl oz) extra virgin olive oil

4 onions, halved and sliced

2 cloves garlic, minced

2 tsps brown sugar

1 tbsp balsamic vinegar

1 egg, lightly beaten

2 tsps water

Beetroot leaves, roughly torn

Preheat oven to 180°C (350°F, Gas Mark 5). Line 2 flat baking trays with baking paper.

In a medium-sized mixing bowl, stir together the goat's cheese, nutmeg, olives and a couple of good grinds of salt and pepper.

Heat the oil in a medium saucepan over medium heat. Add the onion and garlic and sauté for 20 minutes, until the onion is softened.

Add the sugar and vinegar to the onion and cook for another 10 minutes, until the onion is brown and sticky.

Place one of the sheets of the puff pastry on each baking tray. Using a sharp knife score a margin around the edges of each piece of pastry.

Spread equal amounts of the cheese mixture over each sheet. Then spread equal amounts of the onion over the top.

Mix together the egg and the water and brush around the edges of each sheet.

Bake in the oven for 25 minutes, until golden brown on top.

Serve warm or cold, garnished with torn beetroot leaves.

Pumpkin Syrup Pie

A GREAT WAY TO USE UP EXCESS PUMPKIN WHEN IT'S IN
SEASON. THIS PIE IS A SWEET TREAT FOR INDULGENT DAYS

SERVES 12

3 cups (405g, 14oz) pumpkin, peeled and cubed

500g (1lb 2oz) cottage cheese

250g (9oz) cream cheese, cubed, at room temperature

½ cup (180g, 6oz) golden syrup

4 large eggs, at room temperature

1 tsp vanilla extract

2 tsps orange zest

¾ cup (120g, 4oz) brown sugar, firmly packed

2 tbsps almond meal

1 tsp cinnamon

½ tsp allspice

¼ tsp ground ginger

¼ tsp ground cloves

Pinch of salt

Preheat oven to 160°C (325°F, Gas Mark 3) and lightly oil a 23cm (9in) springform cake tin.

Bring a large saucepan of water to the boil. Add the pumpkin and boil for 15 minutes or until the pumpkin has softened. Drain and place in the bowl of a food processor.

Puree until smooth. Remove from the bowl and set aside. You need 1½ cups (340g, 12oz) of pumpkin puree for this recipe.

Add the cottage cheese to the processor and blend until you have a smooth puree.

Using the food processor or an electric mixer, combine the pumpkin mixture with cream cheese, golden syrup, eggs, vanilla, orange zest, sugar, almond meal, spices and salt.

Pour into the cake tin and bake for 1 hour and 10 minutes or until set in the middle.

Let the pie cool in the tin for 1 hour, then place in the fridge for at least 4 hours to cool completely.

Carefully remove from the tin. You may need to run a knife around the edge and underneath to coax it out of the tin.

Serve cold.

Spicy Pumpkin and Walnut Slice

FRAGRANT SPICES AND DELICATE FLAVOURS WARM FROM THE OVEN
ARE A DELIGHT FOR AN AUTUMNAL AFTERNOON TEA

SERVES 8

2 cups (250g, 8oz) flour

1 tsp bicarbonate of soda

¾ tsp salt

1 tsp cinnamon

½ tsp ground ginger

¼ tsp ground nutmeg

¼ tsp ground allspice

250g (9oz) butter, melted

¾ cup (165g, 6oz) honey

½ cup (180g, 6oz) maple syrup

1 egg

2 tsps vanilla extract

1 cup (225g, 8oz) cooked pumpkin, mashed

1 cup (125g, 4oz) walnuts, finely chopped

Preheat oven to 180°C (350°F, Gas Mark 4) and line a 23cm (9in) cake tin with baking paper.

In a large mixing bowl combine flour, bicarb, salt and spices. Set aside.

In a large mixing bowl whisk the melted butter, honey and maple syrup. Add the egg, vanilla and pumpkin and mix well.

Add dry ingredients into wet ingredients, then add the walnuts and blend together with a spatula or metal spoon until fully incorporated.

Scrape batter into tin and bake for 30 minutes or until a skewer inserted in the centre comes out clean.

Remove from oven and cool for 5 minutes in tin before transferring to a wire rack to cool completely.

Zucchini & Quinoa Muffins

MAKES 18

1¼ cups (215g, 8oz) white quinoa

1¼ cups (310ml, 10fl oz) vegetable stock

1 tbsp olive oil

3 medium zucchinis, grated and squeezed

3 tbsps pesto (store-bought or see recipe page 52)

Pinch of freshly ground black pepper

4 large eggs, lightly beaten

¼ cup (25g, 1oz) Parmesan cheese, grated

2 tbsps sesame seeds

Preheat oven to 190°C (375°F, Gas Mark 5). Line a 6-hole muffin tin with muffin cases. Place quinoa and stock in a small saucepan and bring to the boil. Reduce the heat to low and simmer for 20 minutes, until cooked. Heat oil in frying pan over medium-high heat. Add the zucchini and fry for 2 minutes. Remove from heat and place the zucchini in a large mixing bowl. Stir in the pesto, quinoa, pepper, eggs, and Parmesan. Fill the muffin cases with a large dessertspoon-full of mixture. Bake at 20 minutes or until browned on top. Repeat until all the mixture is gone and the muffins are all cooked. Let them cool for 10 minutes before eating. Serve warm scattered with sesame seeds.

Green Pancakes

SERVES 4

1 tsp olive oil

8 cups (240g, 8oz) baby spinach leaves

¾ cup (90g, 3oz) self-raising flour

2 eggs, lightly beaten

¾ cup (185ml, 6fl oz) soy milk

4 tbsps coconut oil, divided

1 tsp ground coriander

½ tsp sea salt

½ tbsp lime zest

1 tsp chopped chives

Heat the oil in a large frying pan over medium heat. Add the spinach in small batches, and cook until wilted. Remove from pan and drain in a colander, pressing down to remove excess liquid. Pat dry with paper towels and chop. Mix the leaves, flour, eggs, soy milk, 2 tablespoons coconut oil, coriander, salt, zest and chives together in a large bowl. Heat the remaining coconut oil in a large frying pan over medium-high heat. Spoon out ¼-cup amounts of the batter into the frying pan. Cook on each side for 3 minutes, until lightly browned. Place the pancakes in a stack on a warm plate while you finish cooking the rest.

SPINACH

Spinach is the leafy green all-star that is celebrated for the high iron content that gives Popeye his muscles. It is also one of the highest-fibre vegetables around — it will balance blood sugar levels, especially when accompanied by sugary sauces or starchy foods that convert quickly to sugar in the bloodstream. Eat it raw in a salad with goat's cheese and a sweet fruit, or throw it in a pan with olive oil and garlic, then mix with cannellini beans for a high-energy comfort dish.

Mozzarella and Spinach Tart

AN ELEGANT AND NUTRITIOUS OPTION THAT IS GREAT SERVED
AS PART OF A BRING-A-PLATE SPREAD

SERVES 4

2 sheets puff pastry

2 tbsps butter

400g (14oz) baby spinach

1 onion, chopped

1 clove garlic, crushed

4 eggs, lightly beaten

1 cup (225g, 8oz) fresh ricotta

¼ cup (60ml, 2fl oz) thickened cream

½ cup (125g, 4oz) Greek yoghurt

1 tsp lemon zest

Pinch of nutmeg

1 tsp salt

Pinch of chilli powder

2 tsps fresh thyme, chopped

200g (7oz) mozzarella balls, sliced into 5mm (¼ in) slices

Sprigs of thyme, to garnish

Preheat oven to 200°C (400°F, Gas Mark 6). Lightly oil a 36 x 13cm (14 x 5in) rectangular quiche tin.

Line the quiche tin with the puff pastry so that it goes up just above the sides by 5mm (¼ in). Prick the bottom and sides with a fork and bake in the oven for 10 minutes. Remove and set aside.

Heat half the butter in a large, deep-sided frying pan over medium heat. Add the spinach in small batches, and cook until wilted. Remove from pan and drain in a colander, pressing down to remove excess liquid. Pat dry with paper towels and roughly chop.

Heat the rest of the butter in the pan and fry the onion and garlic for 4 minutes over medium heat until softened. Remove the onion mix from the pan and set aside for 10 minutes to cool.

Place the onion, spinach, eggs, ricotta, cream, yoghurt, zest, nutmeg, salt, chilli powder and thyme together in a mixing bowl and mix to combine.

Pour the filling over the pastry case and top with slices of mozzarella.

Bake for 50 minutes until the cheese is bubbling and golden brown.

Serve garnished with fresh thyme.

Egg, Chorizo and Cheese Tarts

AN EASY AFTERNOON SNACK THAT THE KIDS WILL LOVE
ASSEMBLING THEMSELVES

MAKES 6 TARTS

1½ sheets puff pastry

¾ cup (90g, 3oz) tasty
cheese, grated

2 large chorizo
sausages, cut into 12
thin slices each

6 eggs

¼ cup (10g, ¼ oz)
parsley leaves, chopped

Preheat oven to 200°C (400°F, Gas Mark 6). Line a large flat
baking tray with lightly oiled baking paper.

Cut the whole sheet of pastry into quarters and the half sheet in
half.

Gently score a line 5mm (¼ in) in from each edge.

Bake in the oven for 10 minutes. Gently push the inside of each
square and it should sink down a little, leaving a 5mm rim
around the edge of each square.

Place a small sprinkling of cheese in each square.

Place a slice of chorizo in each corner.

Break a single egg into the centre of each square.

Bake in the oven for 10 minutes, or until the yolks are cooked
how you like them.

Garnish with chopped parsley.

Vegetable and Bacon Mini Frittatas

A SIMPLE SNACK THAT HITS THE SPOT FOR MORNING TEA.
MAKE IT FIRST THING AND YOU CAN REHEAT IN MINUTES

SERVES 12

8 large eggs

½ cup (125ml, 4fl oz) milk

½ tsp pepper

¼ tsp salt

1 cup (100g, 3½ oz) Parmesan cheese, grated

1 red capsicum, deseeded and chopped

2 small tomatoes, chopped

6 rashers bacon, rind removed, chopped

1 zucchini, chopped

¼ cup (10g, ¼ oz) dill, chopped

Preheat oven to 180°C (350°F, Gas Mark 4).

Grease 12 mini ramekins or two 6-hole large muffin tins.

In a large bowl, whisk together the eggs and milk. Season with salt and pepper.

Add the capsicum, tomato, bacon, zucchini, dill and half the cheese and stir well.

Fill the muffin holes a third of the way with mixture, then sprinkle over the remaining cheese.

Bake for 15 minutes, or until the frittatas puff, are set in the centre and are nice and golden.

KALE

The PR campaign for kale deserves its success — this brassica is robust and leafy, and more flavourful than its cousin, cabbage. It is super-high in calcium and protein and contains a special cholesterol-lowering fibre, which makes it very low on the GI index. Nutritionists recommend at least warming or cooking it to release its nutritional properties. Chefs might massage the leaves, which involves a little water, a little salt, a little time and patient hands — massaging softens the leaves and readies them for sautéing, frying or roasting for a healthy version of chips.

Kale Chips

SERVES 6

1 bunch kale, washed and dried

1 tsp ground cumin

1 tsp paprika

1 tbsp olive oil

2 tsps sea salt

Preheat oven to 175°C (350°F, Gas Mark 4). Line a baking tray.

Remove stems from kale. Cut or tear leaves into bite-sized pieces.

Place in a large bowl, and mix together with the cumin, paprika, oil and salt.

Place on tray and bake for 7 minutes, then remove and turn over.

Bake for a further 7 minutes, until edges of kale are lightly golden, but not burnt.

Serve immediately.

Veggie Chips

SERVES 4

3 beetroots

3 carrots

1 large purple sweet potato

1 large sweet potato

1 cup (250ml, 8fl oz) vegetable oil (for frying)

1 tbsp sea salt

1 tsp ground cumin

1 tsp ground oregano

Heat the oil.

Peel the beetroots, carrots and sweet potatoes and very finely slice into chips (use a mandolin if you have one).

Fry the chips in the hot oil for 2 minutes, stirring to ensure that they are not sticking together.

Remove with a slotted spoon and drain on paper towels.

Season with the salt, cumin and oregano.

LOW CARB FLOURS

Don't give up baking; give up white flour. White flour is great for a special occasion but is refined and converts to glucose in the bloodstream, which we now know leads to sugar rushes and sugar crashes and over time a higher risk of nasties like type 2 diabetes and heart disease.

Of course, there are options. And many.

To get technical, a rule of thumb to follow is: look for flours that fairly evenly balance fibre with carbohydrate. One gram of fibre cancels out the spike effect of one gram of carbohydrates. So if one cup of almond meal contains 2g of carbs and 2g of fibre, this means a win in the carb department.

ALMOND MEAL (OR ALMOND FLOUR): This is actually not flour but almonds that have been ground until they look and feel like flour — and taste lightly nutty and buttery. Almonds are high in protein and calcium and low in carbs — the perfect balance for energy and strength. Almond meal is a little crumblier than regular flour, so it's good to combine it with another low carb flour like polenta, which is made from cornflour and slightly denser. Also, consider an additional egg if the recipe originally calls for white flour. It's best, though, to follow recipes specifically based around almond meal for perfectly moist and fluffy baked goods.

FLAXMEAL: Flaxmeal is not a flour either. It's ground flaxseeds, which can replace both flour and eggs in baking. Confusing? Follow recipes created around flaxseeds, which will usually combine nut milks with another flour, like almond or coconut flour. Flaxseeds are a bit salty and buttery; combined with coconut or almond milk, they become naturally creamy. This all happens without the help of sugar. Flaxseeds are super-high in fibre, vitamin B and protein. They also carry the essential fatty acid called lipoic acid, which is also found in fish and promotes healthy brain function.

COCONUT FLOUR: Coconut flour is high in protein and fibre and tastes, even on its own, already like a sweet baked good. It's also gluten-free. It has just a few more carbs than it has fibre but the nutritional benefits outweigh the mild carbohydrate effects — coconut flour has the vitamin C, vitamin B and iron of the tropical fruit it comes from. It contains 'medium chain fatty acids', which can be more quickly metabolized by the liver than other fats.

LOW CARB BLENDS: Flour blends are a simple option: buy or make blends of almond, coconut, flax, rye, soy, millet and high-fibre oat bran. In a combination of three or more, these flours complement each other in nutritional benefits.

Poppyseed Pie

THIS LUSH POLISH DESSERT IS A LOVELY INDULGENT TREAT FOR ALL THE FAMILY TO ENJOY

SERVES 6

2 cups (290g, 10oz) poppyseeds

2 sheets frozen puff pastry

7 eggs, separated

1 cup (220g, 8oz) stevia sugar replacement

2 cups (240g, 8oz) almond meal

½ cup (80g, 3oz) raisins, chopped

2 tsps orange zest

1 tsp cinnamon

TOPPING

4 tbsps milk

4 tbsps unsalted butter

4 tbsps stevia sugar replacement

4 tbsps cacao powder

Preheat oven to 180°C (350°F, Gas Mark 5). Lightly grease a 23cm (9in) square cake tin.

Place the poppyseeds in a large bowl with boiling water and leave them to soak for at least 4 hours, preferably overnight.

Use cheesecloth or muslin to drain the seeds thoroughly. Place the seeds in a food processor and pulse several times to create a fine mixture.

Place the egg yolks and stevia in a mixer and beat them together until the yolks are pale and thick. Mix through the almond meal, ground poppyseeds, raisins, zest and cinnamon.

In a separate bowl, whisk the egg whites until stiff peaks form. Gently fold into the poppyseed mixture with a slotted spoon.

Place a layer of pastry on the bottom of the cake tin. Prick all over with a fork and bake in the oven for 10 minutes.

Pour the poppyseed mixture into the tin and smooth the top into a flat layer. Place another layer of puff pastry over the top.

Bake in the oven for 50 minutes. Remove and let cool to room temperature.

To make the sauce, mix together the milk, butter and stevia in a small saucepan and bring to a boil. Take off the heat and stir through the cacao powder. Pour over the top layer of pastry. Let the sauce cool before removing the cake from the tin.

Orange and Poppyseed Slice

TURN MORNING TEA INTO HEALTHY FUN FOR EVERYONE WITH THIS BEAUTIFUL LIGHT SLICE

SERVES 8

200g (7oz) butter

2 oranges, peeled, seeds removed and cut into quarters

Zest of 1 orange

3 eggs

½ cup (110g, 4oz) stevia sugar replacement

2½ cups (310g, 10oz) self-raising flour

½ cup (75g, 3oz) poppyseeds

½ cup (125g, 4oz) Greek yoghurt

¼ tsp vanilla extract

Preheat the oven to 180°C (350°F, Gas Mark 4) and line a slice tin.

Place the butter and orange quarters and the orange zest into a bowl and mix with a hand beater (or use an electric mixer) for 2–3 minutes, until light and creamy.

Add eggs, stevia and flour to the bowl and beat for 1 minute. Add the poppyseeds and stir.

Pour mixture into the slice tin and transfer to the oven. Bake for 50 minutes or until it is golden and springy to touch.

Remove from the oven and set on a wire rack to cool.

Mix together the yoghurt and vanilla and drizzle over the cake.

Poppyseed & Lemon Muffins

MAKES 12

2 eggs

¼ cup (90g, 3oz) honey

½ cup (125ml, 4fl oz) milk

¼ cup (60ml, 2fl oz) vegetable oil

1 tbsp lemon juice

1 cup (125g, 4oz) flour

1 cup (125g, 4oz) whole-wheat flour

2 tsps lemon zest

¼ cup (35g, 1¼ oz) poppyseeds

2 tsps cinnamon

¼ tsp cardamom

2 tbsps coconut sugar

2 tsps baking powder

Preheat oven to 200°C (400°F, Gas Mark 6) and grease a 12-hole muffin tin. Place eggs, honey, milk, oil and lemon juice in a bowl and mix. Place flours, zest, poppyseeds, cinnamon, cardamom, coconut sugar, baking powder and pinch of salt into a large bowl and create a well in the centre. Pour wet ingredients into the well and mix until a batter forms. Spoon into the tin, then transfer to the oven and bake for 20 minutes, or until a skewer inserted in the centre comes out clean.

Poppyseed Lemon Pancakes

SERVES 4

2 cups (250g, 8oz) plain flour

1 tbsp baking powder

½ tsp salt

¼ cup (20g, ¾ oz) instant oats

1 tsp lemon zest

3 tbsps poppyseeds

2 eggs, lightly beaten

1¼ cups (310ml, 10fl oz) milk

¼ cup (90g, 3oz) agave syrup

1 tbsp lemon juice

4 tbsps butter, melted

Extra butter, for cooking

Mix flour, baking powder, salt, oats, zest and poppyseeds in a bowl. In a separate bowl, lightly whisk the eggs, milk, agave syrup, lemon juice and melted butter. In batches, pour the wet ingredients into the dry and stir until just combined (still a little lumpy). Melt a small knob of butter in a small frying pan over a low-medium heat. Pour a quarter of the batter into the frying pan and cook until bubbles form on the top of the pancake. Flip onto the other side and continue cooking until golden brown. Serve with a drizzle of honey.

POPPYSEEDS

A spoonful of poppyseeds in any baking or batter mix helps boost the immune system and mellow out sugar highs. These perfect little black seeds are bursting with calcium for bones, zinc for oxygen and iron for muscles, and they also provide an extra boost of fibre to break down glucose in the sugar products that are hard — thought not impossible — to avoid in recipes. Sprinkle poppyseeds on fruit salads and cook them into pancakes to help justify a little extra maple syrup.

Matcha Green Tea Madeleines

A PINCH OF THE GREEN STUFF WILL TRANSFORM THESE CLASSIC
EUROPEAN BISCUITS INTO A SUPERPOWERED TREAT

MAKES 24

140g (5oz) unsalted
butter, melted

140g (5oz) stevia sugar
replacement

1 cup (125g, 4oz) plain
flour

Pinch of sea salt

1 tsp baking powder

1 tbsp matcha powder

1 tbsp milk

½ tsp lemon zest

2 eggs, room
temperature

Sift together into a large bowl the stevia, flour, salt, baking
powder and matcha. Mix to combine and make a well in the
centre.

In a separate bowl, vigorously whisk together the milk, zest
and eggs until bubbles form. Pour the milk mix into the dry
ingredients and stir through.

Stir through half the melted butter. Reserve 1 tablespoon of
the butter, then add the rest to the batter and stir though again.
Do not overmix the butter into the batter. Seal the bowl with
plastic wrap or a lid and store in the fridge for at least 4 hours,
preferably overnight.

Preheat oven to 200°C (400°F, Gas Mark 6).

Melt the reserved butter and use it to butter the moulds of a 12-
hole madeleine tray. Then lightly dust the moulds with flour.

Place 1 tablespoon of the batter into each mould.

Bake for 10 minutes or until the madeleines have risen slightly in
the middle and are cooked through.

Transfer them to a wire rack to cool for a couple of minutes
before eating.

Oatmeal Cookies

SUPER SEEDS, SPICE AND ENERGY-BOOSTING BANANA JUSTIFY
FEELING GOOD WITH EVERY BITE OF THESE YUMMY COOKIES

MAKES 18

1 cup (100g, 3½ oz) banana, mashed

²/₃ cup (160ml, 5fl oz) vegetable oil

1 cup (220g, 8oz) honey

1 egg, beaten

1 tsp ground cinnamon

1 tsp vanilla extract

¼ cup (60ml, 2fl oz) water

1¼ cups (155g, 5oz) plain flour

¼ tsp bicarbonate of soda

Pinch of salt

3½ cups (300g, 10oz) oats

½ cup (60g, 2oz) sunflower seeds

Heat the oven to 180°C (350°F, Gas Mark 4) and line two baking trays with baking paper.

In a large bowl, mix together banana, oil and honey. Gradually beat in the egg and the add cinnamon, vanilla extract and water. Sift the flour, bicarb and a pinch of salt into the bowl.

Place the oats and sunflower seeds in a food processor and pulse several times to roughly chop them. Add the chopped oats and sunflower seeds to the cookie mix and stir through, adding water as needed.

Drop heaped tablespoons of the dough onto baking trays, spaced apart to allow for spread when cooking. Bake for 15 minutes until golden. Leave to cool on the trays for 10 minutes then transfer to a wire rack to cool completely.

Store in an airtight container for up to 3 days.

CASHEWS

Caramel-coloured, bean-shaped nuts, cashews are healthy and indulgent: more buttery than almonds and more flavourful than walnuts when roasted or turned into butter. Cashews are high in vitamin A and super-high in protein. They do, however, come with a health warning: they are higher in fat than other nuts such as walnuts, pistachios and almonds. This isn't cause for cutting them out, however. Much of this fat is good, heart-healthy unsaturated fat. And it's this fat that makes cashews excellent for baking. Cashew butter is higher in protein than regular butter. And cashews can substitute for sweet, caramel flavours without the glucose spike of caramel, which is essentially all sugar.

ROAST YOUR OWN CASHEWS

Skip the extra fat and oil in the packaged roasted nuts and buy them raw. Cashews should be soaked in saltwater for at least 2 hours before roasting; this will soften them, ready the nuts to absorb any seasonings, and also lead to a perfect crunch-to-chew balance. Season with any number of flavours. Cinnamon or nutmeg, maybe a little honey, and salt are winners for sweet nuts. Cumin, curry powder and paprika will create a spicy savoury nut. Roast on a low heat — around 95°C (200°F) — for an hour. Stir every 20 minutes to so they brown evenly.

TASTE TIP: Add roasted cashews to a snack mix of hazelnuts, Brazil nuts and pecans. Season with rosemary, sea salt and brown sugar. These can be dolloped with natural Greek yoghurt for a surprising dessert that seems much sweeter than it is.

MAKE YOUR OWN BUTTER

Grab the nuts and the blender — it's all you need to make creamy cashew butter, although flavourings are good too. Add salt if desired, though without is good for low sodium diets. Take it one step further and add vanilla bean seeds and vanilla extract for a sugar-free sweet spread that can be lathered onto toast — a sweet twist on peanut butter — or melted onto whole-wheat pancakes. Or use the salty vanilla cashew paste for oatmeal cookies with a protein twist.

TASTE TIP: Smear cashew butter over a sliver of banana bread to add salt and natural sugar. Or, get inventive and create a fruity cream biscuit: add the flesh of a passionfruit to cashew butter. Let it soak in so it's moist like cake icing. Smooth it between two plain biscuits, press it together and lick out the salty-sweet ooze.

Black Bean and Coconut Balls

BEANS MEANS THESE LITTLE BOMBSHELLS WILL
ROCK YOUR WORLD!

MAKES 15

²/₃ cup (120g, 4oz) cooked or canned black beans

¾ cup (90g, 3oz) raw cashews, chopped

1½ tbsps coconut oil

¼ cup (20g, ¾ oz) desiccated coconut

2 tbsps cacao powder

½ tbsp maple syrup

Pinch of salt

¼ tsp vanilla extract

Pinch of stevia sugar replacement

¼ cup (30g, 1oz) raw cashews, halved

Drain beans and rinse several times.

Place the beans and chopped cashews in a food processor and pulse a few times to break them up.

Add the rest of the ingredients except the cashew halves and process until the mixture is completely smooth.

Place the mixture in the fridge for at least 4 hours to chill. You need it firm enough to handle.

Divide the mixture into small amounts to make 15 balls. Press a cashew half into each ball and return to the fridge.

These will keep in an airtight container in the fridge for up to 1 week.

Fruit and Oat Vegan Cookies

HEALTHY, SPICY, SWEET AND ALL-ROUND DELICIOUS, THESE ARE A GREAT OPTION FOR LUNCHBOXES

MAKES 10

1 cup (125g, 4oz) buckwheat flour

1 cup (90g, 3oz) instant oats

1 tsp allspice

½ tsp ground cloves

1 ripe banana, mashed

1 apple, cored, peeled and grated

6 dates, pitted and chopped

1 tbsp maple syrup

Preheat oven to 175°C (340°F, Gas Mark 4). Line a large flat baking tray with baking paper.

Mix together the flour, oats and spices in a large bowl and make a well in the centre.

Mix together the banana, grated apple, dates and maple syrup.

Add banana mix to the flour mixture and mix thoroughly.

Place large spoonfuls of the mixture onto the baking tray.

Bake the cookies for 35 minutes until golden brown.

Let them cool for 15 minutes before eating.

These will keep in an airtight container in the fridge for up to 1 week.

Desserts

LOW SUGAR SUBSTITUTES

Low sugar is a phrase on every nutritionist's lips. Yet, there is sugar everywhere. Half the challenge is knowing where to find it, and becoming an expert at reading food labels. Due to its fructose content, white sugar should be avoided as much as possible, but there are many alternatives so sugar cravings need to adapt rather than disappear. Sometimes a little sweetness is just what's needed. For those moments, get to know the other sugars, each with unique flavour qualities and with varying nutritional benefits.

KNOW YOUR SUGAR SUBSTITUTES

STEVIA: Stevia is a herb, processed into a powder or liquid for cooking. It's very sweet, yet it is 100% fructose-free. One teaspoon of stevia equals a cup of old-fashioned sugar.

ERYTHRITOL: Despite its scientific-sounding name, erythritol is a naturally occurring nectar in plants, and fruits and vegetables like grapes and mushrooms.

NATVIA: Natvia is a natural sweetener made by combining the purest and sweetest parts of the stevia plant with erythritol. Natvia is fructose-free.

COCONUT SUGAR: Coconut sugar is nutritious and causes no sugar high and lows. It does have a fructose content on a par with honey and white sugar, so don't overdo it.

MAPLE SYRUP: The sugary sap from the maple tree is delicious, but it contains about 40% fructose so use in moderation.

HONEY: Honey is made up of around 75% sugar. It also has more calories than sugar but is sweeter, so less is needed. Choose organic honey or raw honey, both of which have antioxidant and antibacterial properties. Consider using different flavours — lavender or eucalyptus perhaps, for variety.

Honey and maple syrup are sweeter than sugar, so if you're substituting for sugar in a recipe, use three-quarters of a cup for each cup of sugar. You'll also need to decrease the liquid requirement in the recipe by three tablespoons.

If baking with honey or maple syrup, reduce the oven temperature by 15°C (25°F), since they caramelize and burn faster than granulated sweeteners.

RICE MALT SYRUP (ALSO KNOWN AS BROWN RICE SYRUP): Made from boiling brown rice, rice malt syrup is gluten- and wheat-free and also fructose-free — a winner! It has a mild butterscotch flavour. Pour it into milk, sweeten up cereal, and indulge in a batch of muffins!

Key Lime Cheesecake

EVERY NOW AND THEN YOU NEED A TREAT: THIS RICH,
CREAMY AND ZESTY CHEESECAKE FITS THE BILL

MAKES 8

GINGER SNAP BASE

30 sugar-free ginger
snap biscuits

5 tbsps butter, melted

1 tsp allspice

CHEESECAKE FILLING

450g (1lb) cream
cheese, softened

1 tbsp maple syrup

½ cup (125g, 4oz) sour
cream

½ cup (125ml, 4fl oz)
thickened cream

2 tbsps lime zest

¼ cup (60ml, 2fl oz)
fresh lime juice

CREAM

1 cup (250ml, 8fl oz)
whipping cream

2 tbsps honey (optional)

½ tsp vanilla extract

To make the base, place the ginger snap biscuits in a blender and
process until a rough crumb forms. Pour into a bowl, add butter
and allspice, and stir to combine.

Press biscuit mixture into the base of a greased 23 x 4cm
(9 x 1.5in) cake tin and refrigerate for at least 1 hour.

Using an electric mixer, beat cream cheese and maple syrup
together.

Mix through the sour cream, thickened cream, 1 tablespoon lime
zest and lime juice until smooth

Smooth the cheesecake mixture over the base and place in the
fridge for at least 4 hours to set.

To make the whipped cream, you need things to be cold. Place
the mixer bowl and whisk in the freezer for at least 20 minutes to
chill. Pour whipping cream, honey (if using) and vanilla into the
cold bowl and whisk on high speed for 1 minute until medium
to stiff peaks form. Don't overbeat.

Top the cake with the cream and the remaining lime zest to
decorate.

Apple Bread and Butter Pudding

A COSY, COMFORTING TREAT THAT'S REASSURINGLY FAMILIAR.
SOURDOUGH BREAD IS THE HEALTHIEST CHOICE FOR THIS DESSERT

SERVES 6

2 large apples, peeled, cored and sliced (use sundowner or gala)

½ cup (80g, 3oz) sultanas

¼ cup (60g, 2oz) agave syrup

10 large, thick bread slices (preferably sourdough)

2½ cups (625ml, 20fl oz) almond milk

2 tsps vanilla essence

3 eggs, lightly beaten

2 tsps lemon zest

1 tsp allspice

½ tsp cinnamon

¼ cup (90g, 3oz) honey

Preheat oven to 160°C (325°F, Gas Mark 3). Lightly grease a 2L (4pt) capacity casserole dish.

Place the apple slices, sultanas and agave syrup in a small saucepan over medium heat. Gently cook for 5 minutes, until the apples have softened.

Cut all the bread slices in half.

Arrange a layer of bread slices in the bottom of the dish, then a layer of the apple mixture. Repeat until you end up with a top layer of bread slices.

Whisk together the rest of the ingredients, except the honey, in a large bowl.

Pour over the bread and apples mix. Push down on the top to ensure the bread is soaking up the liquid.

Drizzle the honey over the top.

NOTE: Choosing sourdough bread is best for low sugar diets. The process of fermentation releases lactic acid, which helps the body digest food and gives a leg-up to the good bacteria in the gut. Also, research has shown that it doesn't cause the same spike in blood sugar levels as ordinary white bread.

Pear Pie with Cinnamon

SERVES 8

6 tbsps unsalted butter, cubed

4 tbsps honey

1 egg, lightly beaten

¾ cup (90g, 3oz) almond meal

2 tsps lemon juice

1 tsp water

1 tbsp cornflour

3 firm pears, cored and thinly sliced

1 tbsp coconut sugar

1 tsp cinnamon

Preheat oven to 190°C (375°F, Gas Mark 5), grease a 20cm (8in) pie dish. Beat together butter, 3 tablespoons of the honey and a pinch of salt until light and fluffy. Mix in egg then almond meal. Press mixture into pie dish and chill in the fridge for 30 minutes. Combine 1 tablespoon honey, juice, water and cornflour in a saucepan over low heat for 3 minutes. Add pear slices and gently stir to coat. Arrange slices over crust, pushing firmly into the base. Pour rest of the syrup over the top. Bake for 35 minutes, until golden brown. Remove from oven and cool for 10 minutes.Serve warm with coconut sugar and cinnamon dusted over top.

Baked Pears with Fruit & Nut

SERVES 4

2 large ripe pears, halved and cored

¼ tsp cinnamon

¼ tsp allspice

¼ cup (30g, 1oz) walnuts, chopped

¼ cup (30g, 1oz) almonds, chopped

¼ cup (40g, 1½ oz) dried cranberries, chopped

1 tbsp raw honey

2 tsps lemon juice

¼ cup (60ml, 2fl oz) hot water

Mint leaves, to garnish

Preheat oven to 180°C (350°F, Gas Mark 5). Line a large flat baking tray with baking paper. Place the pear halves, cut side up, on the baking tray. Toss together the spices, nuts and cranberries then spoon portions of the mix on top of the pears. In a small bowl, mix together the honey, lemon juice and water. Drizzle the honey mixture over the pears. Bake in the oven for 30 minutes, or until the pears are softened. Serve hot with fresh mint leaves for garnish.

PEARS

If you are watching your sugar intake, pears are a good enough choice of fruit. They have a low score on the GI index thanks to a healthy ratio of sugar to fibre content. Eat with the skin on to get the full benefit of the fibre. Pears canned in syrup will contain more sugar, so remember to check the label. Otherwise, kick back and enjoy the meltingly sweet, succulent fruit that Europeans have nicknamed 'butter fruit' in some varieties.

Lemon Cake with Cashew Frosting

A GLUTEN-FREE TREAT THAT'S SWEET, TANGY, CREAMY AND DELICIOUS

SERVES 8-10

CAKE

½ cup (125ml, 4fl oz) almond milk

3 tbsps lemon juice

1 cup (220g, 8oz) stevia sugar replacement

2 tbsps lemon zest

½ cup (125ml, 4fl oz) coconut oil

3 eggs, room temperature

½ tsp vanilla extract

2 cups (240g, 8oz) almond meal

1½ tsps baking powder

¼ tsp bicarbonate of soda

½ tsp salt

FROSTING

2¼ cups (280g, 10oz) cashews, soaked for 2 hours

1-2 tbsps lemon juice

2 tbsps coconut oil

⅓ cup (115g, 4oz) maple syrup

Water, as needed

2 tsps lemon zest to garnish

Preheat oven to 180°C (350°F, Gas Mark 5). Lightly grease a 23 x 4cm (9 x 1.5in) cake tin.

Combine the lemon juice and milk and let sit for 10 minutes.

Combine the lemon zest and sugar. Beat together the sugar and coconut oil until thoroughly mixed. Then add the eggs, one at a time, until thoroughly combined. Whisk in the milk and the vanilla extract.

In a large mixing bowl, mix the almond meal, baking powder, bicarb and salt and make a well in the centre. Add the wet ingredients to the dry and stir until combined.

Pour into the cake tin and bake for 40 minutes, or until a skewer inserted into the middle comes out clean. Let it sit for 15 minutes before turning out onto a wire rack to cool.

Place all the frosting ingredients in a high-speed blender and blend until smooth, adding a small amount of water, just enough to hold the frosting together.

Once the cake is at room temperature, spread the frosting over the cake and sprinkle the remaining lemon zest over the top.

BERRIES

Is there anything sweeter — in every way — than a bowl of fresh berries? Bursts of red, blue and purple straight from wild bushes; strawberries, raspberries, blackberries and perfectly round blueberries need nothing but themselves. It's all natural. And, for the most part, all on the healthy end of the fructose-to-fibre spectrum. While bananas, mangoes, cherries and grapes all skew high on the fructose end of the scale — these have more sugar than fibre — berries are relatively low in fructose and have equal fibre levels to massage the sugar spike into the system.

Some berries have more sugar than others. Raspberries are a winner, with 5g of sugar and 8g of fibre in one cup of the perfect fruit, which means the fructose will do just what it's supposed to do without a later crash. Strawberries have 7g of sugar and all the vitamin C a healthy body needs for a day. And those delicious, seedy blackberries pretty much balance 7g of sugar with 8g of fibre.

But it isn't all about sugar. Nutritionists sing the praises of berries all year long — berries are a wonder food in many diets and can help weight loss. They can be eaten in any season as snap-frozen berries are just as good as fresh — in fact, sometimes they're even better, as they retain the full nutrients whereas fresh berries start deteriorating as the days go by.

BERRY BENEFITS

BALANCING BLOOD SUGAR: A side of strawberries with a meal will break down starches into simple sugar, which means that the bloodstream receives less sugar and more nutrients. Berries are excellent for lowering blood sugar and preventing insulin from converting sugar into fat. This is ideal for preventing type 2 diabetes and helping with weight loss.

ANTIOXIDANTS: A handful of berries eaten fresh or added to oatmeal can boost the immune system and deliver powerful antioxidant benefits. Antioxidants are like cell warriors, protecting against damage from natural elements as well as harmful substances in the diet. Antioxidants are thought to help slow the ageing processes and prevent common and chronic diseases like cancer and heart disease. Research has also shown that people with high antioxidants in their diets tend to weigh less.

METABOLISM BOOSTERS: A handful of raspberries delivers ketones into the bloodstream, a compound that kick-starts the metabolism and helps carve into body fat. This is good for the waistline and is thought to play a role in preventing heart disease, type 2 diabetes and certain cancers. (So add berries to the bowl of cream and proceed, guilt-free.)

Semolina Raspberry Cake

THIS CAKE IS A FANTASTIC CHOICE FOR CAKE LOVERS LOOKING TO INDULGE WITHOUT THE UNPLEASANT SUGAR RUSH

SERVES 8–10

2 eggs, separated, room temperature

30g (1oz) unsalted butter, room temperature

¼ cup (90g, 3oz) maple syrup

2 tsps lemon zest

1 cup (250g, 9oz) Greek yoghurt

250g (9oz) fine semolina

2 tsps baking powder

1 tsp vanilla extract

200g (7oz) frozen raspberries

100g (3½ oz) fresh raspberries, for serving

1 tbsp stevia icing sugar

Mint leaves, to garnish

Preheat oven to 175°C (340°F, Gas Mark 4). Grease a 23 x 4cm (9 x 1.5in) pie dish.

Beat together the egg yolks, butter and maple syrup until light and fluffy. Mix through the lemon zest, then stir through the yoghurt.

Mix together the semolina and baking powder in a large bowl and make a well in the centre. Add the yoghurt mixture and stir until just combined.

Whisk the egg whites and vanilla extract until stiff peaks form. Gently fold the whites into the cake mix using a slotted spoon.

Pour half the cake mix into the dish, then dot with half the frozen raspberries. Pour the rest of the batter over the top. Push the remaining frozen raspberries into the top of the cake.

Bake the cake for 1 hour 10 minutes, or until golden and a skewer inserted into the middle comes out clean.

Let the cake sit for 15 minutes before turning out onto a wire rack to cool. Serve with fresh raspberries and dust the top with the icing sugar; add a couple of mint leaves for garnish.

Soufflé with Blueberries

COTTAGE CHEESE IS KEY TO TRANSFORMING THIS CLASSIC FRENCH DISH INTO A LOW SUGAR, HEALTHY TREAT

SERVES 12

SOUFFLÉ

125g (4oz) salted butter, room temperature

$1/3$ cup (70g, 2½ oz) stevia sugar replacement

6 large eggs, room temperature, separated

1 cup (250g, 9oz) sour cream

1 cup (250g, 9oz) Greek yoghurt

¼ cup (60ml, 2fl oz) orange juice

1 cup (125g, 4oz) plain flour

1 tsp cinnamon

2 tsps baking powder

FILLING

225g (8oz) cream cheese, room temperature, cubed

2 cups (450g, 1lb) cottage cheese

2 egg yolks

3 tbsps agave syrup

1 tsp lemon zest

1 tsp vanilla extract

3 cups (300g, 10oz) frozen blueberries

¾ cup (75g, 3oz) redcurrants

TOPPING

2 tbsps stevia icing sugar

Mint leaves, to garnish

Preheat oven to 180°C (350°F, Gas Mark 5). Grease a large 18cm (7in) soufflé dish or 12 small soufflé ramekins.

To make the filling, beat the cream cheese until light and fluffy. Add the cottage cheese, egg yolks, agave, zest and vanilla and beat again until well blended and smooth. Gently stir in half the blueberries and redcurrants. Set aside.

To make the soufflé mix, whisk together the butter and sugar until light and fluffy. Whisk in the egg yolks, until they're creamy and pale. Then stir in the sour cream, yoghurt and juice.

Mix together the flour, cinnamon and baking powder in a large bowl and make a well in the centre. Pour the sour cream mixture into the dry ingredients and stir until just combined.

Whisk the egg whites until stiff peaks form. Gently fold into the soufflé batter using a slotted spoon. Be as gentle as possible when handling the soufflé mix from now on, to keep as much air in it as you can.

Pour half the soufflé mix into the soufflé dish. Then spoon the filling over the top. Spread the rest of the soufflé mix over the top of this.

Bake in the oven for 50 minutes until light and fluffy and golden on top.

Serve hot topped with remaining blueberries and redcurrants, and a dusting of icing sugar with mint leaves for garnish.

Blackberry Mousse

SERVES 4

400g (14oz) fresh blackberries

⅓ cup (70g, 2½ oz) stevia sugar replacement

2½ gelatin leaves

2 ⅓ cups (600ml, 20fl oz) thickened cream

2 egg whites

Extra berries, to garnish

Mint leaves, to garnish

Heat the blackberries and sugar with one-third cup (80ml, 3fl oz) water in a medium saucepan over medium heat for 20 minutes until the sugar is dissolved. Don't let it boil. Remove from the heat.

Soften the gelatin in cold water for 10 minutes. Squeeze the leaves to remove excess water and add to the blackberries. Stir until they are dissolved. Place in the fridge for at least 3 hours to cool.

Whip the cream until stiff. Stir through the blackberry mix until combined. Whisk the egg whites until stiff peaks form. Gently fold into the mousse mixture.

Spoon into serving bowls or glasses then place in fridge for at least 2 hours to set. Serve with a couple of fresh berries on top and mint leaves.

Berry Yoghurt Parfait

SERVES 4

2 cups (400g, 14oz) fresh strawberries, chopped

2 cups (290g, 10oz) fresh blackberries

1 tsp fresh mint, chopped

2 tbsps maple syrup

225g (8oz) mascarpone cheese

1 cup (250g, 9oz) Greek yoghurt

1 tsp vanilla extract

1 cup (145g, 5oz) blackberries to garnish

Heat the strawberries, blackberries, mint and maple syrup in a medium saucepan over low heat for 30 minutes until the fruit has softened. Stir to break up the berries. Remove from heat and cool in the fridge for at least 2 hours.

Whisk the mascarpone, yoghurt and vanilla together until thoroughly combined and smooth.

Alternate layers of the cheese mix and berry mix in each dessert glass or bowl, finishing with the cheese mixture on top. Place in the fridge for at least 30 minutes to set.

Serve with fresh berries on top and mint to garnish.

BLACKBERRIES

Blackberries have a special kind of sweetness. They are one of the healthiest fruits around, delivering more fibre and antioxidants than sugar. Their juicy bite-sized selves can help lower blood sugar and have been shown to help slow ageing and prevent inflammation that leads to common chronic conditions. Bake them into muffins or stew up with coconut and cinnamon and pour over pancakes. A surprise treat is fresh blackberries smothering a wheel of Brie or Camembert — it's a party appetizer or as good a dessert as any.

Berry Tart with a Walnut Crust

A SUMMER SUPER-FRUIT DELIGHT THAT'S COMPLETELY GUILT-FREE
AND SO EASY TO PUT TOGETHER

SERVES 8

CRUST

2 cups (310g, 10oz) walnuts

1 tsp bicarbonate of soda

¼ tsp salt

2 tbsps coconut oil, melted

FILLING

2 tbsps cornflour

1 tbsp cold water

4 cups (400g, 14oz) fresh or frozen blueberries

2 tbsps lemon juice

1 tsp stevia sugar replacement

1 tsp vanilla extract

Preheat oven to 175°C (350°F, Gas Mark 4). Lightly grease a 27cm (10.5in) tart tin.

To make the crust, blend walnuts, bicarb and salt in a food processor until finely ground. Add coconut oil and pulse to combine.

Spread the crumb to line the tart tin and press firmly.

Transfer to the oven to bake for 15 minutes. Remove from oven and set aside to cool.

For the filling, mix cornflour and water together in a small bowl to make a slurry.

Place blueberries, lemon juice, stevia and vanilla extract in a saucepan over a low-medium heat. Stir in cornflour slurry and simmer until sauce thickens.

Refrigerate for 1 hour.

Spoon the berry filling into the baked tart crust. Chill in the fridge until ready to serve.

CREAM

Fat is not the enemy. (Fructose is.) Sugar-free does not have to mean lactose-free for people who can tolerate dairy. Scientists and nutritionists are learning that the path to healthy eating is about a balanced diet, and understanding the ways our bodies process the balance of calories, fat, sugar and nutrients that occur in natural and processed foods.

It's also about indulgence and motivation. Deprivation does little good, especially when trying to form new habits. This is excellent news for those on the healthy, low sugar path who would like to continue licking the whipped cream bowl, long after everyone else has left the kitchen.

Well, licking the bowl might be going a bit far. Yet, like butter and milk, cream is an indulgent, calcium-rich and useful ingredient in all sorts of cooking — sometimes it's a splash in a sauce for an Italian dinner. And cream almost always elevates a dessert into the luxury realm.

Contrary to some wisdom, going full fat is considered the healthiest choice. Increasingly, research shows no evidence that low fat dairy products are healthier and that they might in fact be less healthy. Low fat options have gone through extra processing and may contain lower protein levels, which is key to allowing the body to digest the fat. And there are many brands that contain preservatives and additives as well as sugar. If opting for low fat dairy, it's important to check labels.

Significantly, evidence shows that full fat dairy can lower the rates of obesity, type 2 diabetes and heart disease. Butter is rich in short- and medium-chain fatty acids, which help lower harmful cholesterols and help prevent certain cancers. Full fat butter and cream is an excellent source of vitamins A, D and K, which are essential for absorbing calcium.

WHIPPED CREAM TRICKS

Use heavy (thickened) cream. Start with chilled cream — this keeps the fat fresh for longer, for silkier, fluffier cream. Also, try to start with cold tools: a cold mixing bowl and electric mixer. It can be easy to over-whip cream, which leads to a dense white mass that is halfway to butter. Dare to whip it by hand with a whisk. Or, use an electric beater but stop just as the texture begins to change. Whisk the rest by hand to take it to light, silky folds.

Try adding Greek yoghurt to cream: this is lower in calories, higher in protein, and actually tastes a little lighter and tangier, as though sugar has been added.

For 'sweet' flavoured creams, try cocoa, cardamom and vanilla extract; dashes of maple syrup, dark rum and allspice; or coconut and cinnamon.

Victoria Layer Cake with Cream and Raspberries

SERVES 10

3 large eggs, at room temperature, separated

1²/₃ cups (205g, 7oz) light buckwheat flour

1²/₃ cups (205g, 7oz) gluten-free plain flour

3 tsps baking powder

1 tsp sea salt

2 tsps ground allspice

3 tsps orange zest

300g (3½ oz) honey

¾ cup (185ml, 6fl oz) coconut oil

¾ cup (185ml, 6fl oz) almond milk

1¼ cups (300ml, 10fl oz) whipping cream

1¼ cups (300ml, 10fl oz) coconut cream

2 tsps vanilla extract

½ cup (115g, 4oz) sugar-free raspberry jam

2 cups (250g, 8oz) fresh raspberries

Preheat oven to 180°C (350°F, Gas Mark 5). Line a rectangle cake pan with heavily greased baking paper.

Beat the egg whites until stiff peaks form. Set aside.

In a large mixing bowl, combine the flours, baking powder, salt, allspice and zest. Make a well in the centre.

Whisk together the egg yolks and honey until they're light and creamy. Slowly whisk in the coconut oil until well combined.

Add to the dry ingredients and mix through. Gradually add the almond milk until fully combined. Gently fold the egg whites in with a slotted spoon until just combined.

Pour a third of the cake mix into the pan and bake in the oven for 20 minutes, or until a skewer inserted into the middle comes out clean. Remove from the oven and let cool on a wire rack.

Remove cake from tin, and repeat baking with the remaining mixture to form the three layers of the cake. Ensure the baking paper is greased each time before filling with the next batch of cake batter.

Whip the creams with the vanilla extract until stiff peaks form.

Spread half the jam over the top of one of the cake rectangles and then spread a third of the cream over the top. Repeat with the second cake rectangle and place on top of the first. Place the third cake rectangle on top of the second and spread the rest of the cream on top.

Place in the fridge to help the cream set. Serve with fresh raspberries on top.

Strawberry Cream Parfait

A FAST AND COLOURFUL DESSERT THAT'S PERFECT FOR LAZY SUMMER EVENINGS

SERVES 2

STRAWBERRY LAYER

1 cup (200g, 7oz) fresh strawberries, chopped

2 tsps pure maple syrup

CREAM LAYER

½ cup (125g, 4oz) Greek yoghurt

60g (2oz) mascarpone

1 tbsp coconut cream (don't shake the can, use the thick cream at the top)

1 tsp vanilla extract

3 tbsps agave syrup

Pinch of salt

4 strawberries, halved

BISCUIT LAYER

2 finger biscuits, crumbled

1 sugar-free ginger biscuit, crumbled

Place the strawberries and maple syrup in a small saucepan and gently cook for 20 minutes over low heat, just enough to soften the strawberries so they release some juice. Remove from heat and set aside to cool.

Whip together the yoghurt, mascarpone, coconut ream, vanilla extract, agave and salt until smooth and thickened.

To assemble, place half the crumbled biscuits in the bottom of 2 dessert glasses or small bowls. Spoon a portion of the cream over the biscuits, then half the strawberry mixture. Top with the rest of the cream and then place the fresh strawberry halves on top.

Ice Cream Sandwiches

MAKES 6

COOKIES

1 large egg white

2 tbsps honey

¼ tsp salt

1 tsp cinnamon

1 tsp vanilla extract

1 tsp baking powder

¾ cup (90g, 3oz) almond flour

½ cup (40g, 1½ oz) desiccated coconut

1 cup (90g, 3oz) oats

3 tbsp coconut oil (melted)

ICE CREAM

3 eggs separated

1¼ cups (280ml, 9fl oz) whipping cream

80g (3oz) xylitol

3 tsp vanilla extract

ALMOND CRUST

½ cup (60g, 2oz toasted almonds, crushed

Preheat oven to 160°C (325°F, Gas Mark 3) and line a baking sheet with baking paper.

Place the egg white, honey, salt, cinnamon and vanilla in the bowl of a stand mixer and mix to combine the ingredients. Add the baking powder, almond flour, desiccated coconut and oats, and stir to combine, then add coconut oil and incorporate fully.

Spoon 12 tablespoons of the mixture onto the prepared baking tray and flatten. Transfer to the oven to bake for 15 minutes until golden. Remove from the oven and, for perfectly round cookies, use a cookie cutter when still warm to trim off the edges. Cool for 5 minutes on the baking sheet before placing on a wire rack to cool completely.

Meanwhile, make the ice cream. Whisk the egg yolks in a bowl until pale and creamy. Set aside. In another bowl, whisk egg whites to stiff peaks. Add half the xylitol then whisk again until stiff peaks form. Set aside. In a third bowl, whip the cream to soft peaks, then, and fold in the other ingredients, including the remaining xylitol. Transfer ice cream mixture into a tub and freeze for at least 2 hours before assembling the sandwiches.

To assemble, place a dollop of ice cream on one cookie and sandwich with another cookie. Use a palette knife (or an ordinary knife will do the job) to scrape a neat edge around the ice cream, then roll the sides in the almond crust. Repeat with the remaining cookies.

VANILLA PODS

Everything seems to start from vanilla — from ice cream to milkshakes to the classic birthday sponge cake. It's also lurking in savoury dishes such as buttery French sauces, fragrant curries and stews.

Vanilla comes from a tropical flower, a gorgeous cream- or sometimes lemon-coloured orchid that does the world a favour when it blossoms one day of the year — that's it, there's one day a year when vanilla beans can be pollinated. On that day, bees are busy in parts of France, Mexico, Tahiti and Africa. This explains something about why vanilla can be expensive — it's a rare jewel that every chef and home cook is clamouring for. Vanilla is one item to splurge on, and the thing is: kept in a cool, dry place, it'll last for almost a lifetime.

KNOW YOUR VANILLA

VANILLA ESSENCE: It can be tempting to grab the most affordable bottle off the shelf in the baking aisle, however vanilla essence is usually highly processed and contains only a tiny bit of vanilla. Vanilla essence can leave a bitter aftertaste if any flavour even makes it through the cooking process.

VANILLA EXTRACT: Vanilla extract takes the form of a golden brown liquid and is the most commonly used vanilla. It's made by pulverising vanilla beans in an alcohol-water solution, which is then aged. Tip: add vanilla extract to mixtures that are slightly cooled, not piping hot, as heat weakens the flavour.

DIY VANILLA EXTRACT: Add vanilla pods to an airtight jar full of 80-proof alcohol like rum, vodka or bourbon. Leave to infuse for at least a month. Remove the pods when the vanilla tastes as intense as desired.

VANILLA PODS: Vanilla pods are also known as vanilla beans — these are the pure vanilla, straight from the orchid. Pods are finger-long, black and fibrous and they've usually been sun-dried for preservation. They can be chopped finely and thrown in the blender along with smoothie ingredients or cake mix. Or split the pod open with a sharp knife, scoop out the lush, dark little seeds from the inside and add to salad dressings, muffin batters or the velvety cream mixture for a creme caramel.

VANILLA PASTE: Vanilla paste combines vanilla extract with seeds from the vanilla pod. The paste is often thickened with a natural thickener. It is not necessarily more concentrated than a liquid extract, yet it contains the vanilla seeds, which add extra crunch and fragrance to cupcakes, stewed peaches or creme brulee.

Panna Cotta with Fresh Berries

THIS TAKE ON THE ITALIAN CLASSIC IS EASY TO MAKE, AND
EVERY MOUTHFUL PROVIDES JUST AS MUCH CREAMY GOODNESS

SERVES 4

1 cup (250ml, 8fl oz) tinned coconut cream (don't shake the tin when you open it and use all the thick solid in the top of the can)

1 cup (250ml, 8fl oz) almond milk

$1/3$ cup (115g, 4oz) agave syrup

2 tsps gelatin powder

2 tsps pure vanilla extract

1 tbsp strained fresh orange juice

1 cup (200g, 7oz) fresh strawberries, chopped

¼ cup (25g, 1oz) fresh blueberries

Mint leaves, to garnish

Heat the cream and milk in a saucepan over medium-low heat for 4 minutes.

Add the agave and gelatin and stir constantly until the gelatin is dissolved. Don't let it boil — reduce the heat if necessary.

Once the gelatin is thoroughly absorbed, stir through the vanilla and orange juice.

Pour the mixture evenly into each dessert glass or jar and then seal with plastic wrap.

Refrigerate for at least 4 hours, preferably overnight.

To serve, top with chopped strawberries and blueberries and garnish with fresh mint.

Vegan Chocolate Cake with Cashew Cream

CHICKPEAS, CASHEWS, TOFU — THIS IS NOT YOUR USUAL CHOCOLATE CAKE! BUT THIS SWEET, INTENSE TREAT IS WELL WORTH THE EFFORT

SERVES 8

2 cups (480g, 1lb 1oz) cooked chickpeas, rinsed and drained

1/3 cup (80ml, 3fl oz) fresh orange juice

2 tsps vanilla extract

1 cup (260g, 9oz) silken tofu, whipped until smooth and light

1 tsp cinnamon

1 tsp allspice

1 cup (220g, 8oz) stevia sugar replacement

1/4 cup (30g, 1oz) raw cacao powder

1/2 tsp baking powder

1/4 tsp bicarbonate of soda

Pinch of salt

1 cup (175g, 6oz) dairy-free dark chocolate, finely chopped

250g (9oz) fresh strawberries

Mint leaves, to garnish

CASHEW CREAM

3 cups (375g, 13oz) cashews

2 tbsps lemon juice

3 tbsps coconut oil

1/2 cup (180g, 6oz) maple syrup

1 tsp vanilla extract

Water, as needed

To make the cashew cream, soak the cashews in a bowl of water overnight. Strain the cashews and place in a blender with the lemon juice, oil, maple syrup and vanilla extract, and as much water as needed to puree until smooth. Place in the fridge for at least 1 hour to firm up.

Preheat oven to 180°C (350°F, Gas Mark 4). Line a small 16cm (6in) cake tin with baking paper. You'll need to have more baking paper on hand.

In a medium-sized mixing bowl, mix together the cinnamon, allspice, sugar, cacao, baking powder, bicarb and salt. Set aside.

Place the chickpeas and orange juice in a food processor and blend until smooth.

Blend in the vanilla and tofu in small portions, giving a few good pulses after each addition to mix thoroughly.

Add the dry ingredients to the chickpea mix and blend until mixed thoroughly. Scrape down the sides of the bowl as needed to ensure everything is combined.

Remove the mixture from the processor and stir through the chocolate. Pour one-third of the cake mix into the cake tin.

Bake for 30 minutes or until a skewer inserted into the middle comes out clean. Let the cake sit for 15 minutes in the tin until removing to a wire rack.

Repeat with the other two-thirds of the cake mix until you have 3 round, cooled cake layers.

To assemble, spread one-third of the cashew cream on top of one cake layer, repeat with the other two cakes and the rest of the cream. Stack the cakes on top of each other. Serve with fresh strawberries and mint leaves to garnish.

Baked Apples & Mascarpone

SERVES 6

2½ cups (460g, 1lb) mascarpone cheese

3 tbsps honey

1 tsp vanilla extract

6 apples (such as sundowner or gala)

4 tbsps walnuts, chopped

4 tbsps hazelnuts, chopped

1 tsp cinnamon

¼ cup (60g, 2oz) butter

2 tbsps stevia icing sugar

Preheat oven to 200°C (400°F, Gas Mark 6) and grease a deep oven dish with a lid.

Place mascarpone, honey and vanilla in a large mixing bowl and stir to loosely combine.

Remove the core from each apple and slice into wedges. Place the apples into the prepared dish and sprinkle with walnuts, hazelnuts, cinnamon and a knob of butter. Cover and bake in the oven for 30 minutes until apples are very soft.

Remove apples from oven and spoon the mascarpone honey mixture over the top. Dust with icing sugar and serve hot.

Vanilla Custard

SERVES 2

1²/₃ cups (400ml, 13fl oz) almond milk

2 eggs

2 tbsps cornflour

½ tbsp stevia sugar replacement

½ vanilla pod, scraped

Whisk together the eggs, stevia and cornflour until smooth. Add the milk, a third at a time, whisking constantly to keep it smooth.

Pour the mixture into a saucepan and gently heat over medium. Whisk constantly until boiling to prevent lumps forming.

Add the vanilla and stir through. Reduce heat to low and simmer for 3 minutes, still stirring. Add more stevia if needed.

Serve warm or cold.

HOME - MADE
APPLE CIDER

Apples are among the sweetest fruits with a high fibre content — the bulk of which is in the peel. Raw and organic apple juice and cider is full of vitamins A and C, especially when made at home without additives. Many recipes will recommend starting with store-bought juice and spicing it up with nutmeg, cinnamon and honey. It's better to start from scratch: choose organic, sweet apples like fuji, gala or honeycrisp. Throw cinnamon sticks, nutmeg, cloves and whole apples in boiling water for 1 hour, then simmer for 2 hours. Let stand for an hour or so more, then strain through a fine mesh strainer or cheesecloth. Allow bits of pulp through for extra antioxidants or strain until clear for a smooth, naturally sweet concoction.

Chocolate Irish Cream Dessert

THE PERFECT CONCLUSION TO A LONG DAY OR A LAZY DINNER PARTY WITH FRIENDS. THIS DESSERT IS A CHEEKY SURPRISE

SERVES 8

CHOCOLATE MOUSSE & PEANUT BUTTER MOUSSE

4 eggs, separated

4 cups (1L, 2pt) plus ½ cup (125ml, 4fl oz) whipping cream

100g (3½ oz) sugar-free dark chocolate, chopped

3 tbsps raw cacao powder

4 tbsps stevia sugar replacement

1 cup (250g, 9oz) smooth peanut butter (or crunchy if you like)

IRISH CREAM

1½ cups (375ml, 13fl oz) whipping cream

½ vanilla pod, scraped

½ tsp stevia sugar replacement

8 tbsps Bailey's Irish Cream liqueur

TO SERVE

¼ cup (30g, 1oz) peanuts, finely chopped

¼ cup (45g, 1½ oz) dark sugar-free chocolate, finely chopped

Whisk the egg whites until stiff peaks form, divide in half and set aside.

Heat the ½ cup of cream gently over low heat until almost simmering. Remove immediately from the heat. Set aside half the warmed cream and stir the rest with the chocolate, cacao and 2 tablespoons of stevia. Stir until the chocolate is melted then set aside.

Whip the 4 cups of cream until stiff peaks form. Divide in half, setting one portion aside, then gently fold the chocolate mixture into the other portion.

Fold one half of the egg whites carefully into the chocolate mixture until just mixed through. Spoon the chocolate mousse evenly into 8 dessert glasses and place in the fridge.

To make the peanut butter mousse, stir the rest of the heated cream into the peanut butter along with the rest of the stevia. Gently fold the rest of the whipped cream into the peanut butter mixture until just mixed. Fold the remaining egg whites gently into the peanut butter mixture.

Spoon the peanut butter mousse evenly over the chocolate mousse in each of the glasses. Return the glasses to the fridge to chill.

To make the Irish cream, whip the cream with the vanilla pod scrapings until thickened to your preference. Add the Bailey's Irish Cream liqueur and stir to combine.

Top the dessert glasses with the cream and return to the fridge for at least 3 hours to set.

Top with a sprinkling of peanuts and chocolate.

Black Bean Brownie with Pistachio Ice Cream

IT'S HARD TO BELIEVE THIS LUSCIOUS, RICH AND GOOEY
BROWNIE IS FULL OF ENERGY-BOOSTING SUPERFOODS

SERVES 10

BROWNIE

1 x 400g (14oz) can
black beans

2 tbsps raw cacao
powder

½ cup (40g, 1½ oz)
quick oats

¼ tsp salt

⅓ cup (115g, 4oz)
maple syrup

Pinch of stevia sugar
replacement

¼ cup (60ml, 2fl oz)
coconut oil, melted

2 tsps vanilla extract

½ tsp baking powder

1 cup (175g, 6oz)
sugar-free dark
chocolate, shaved

ICE CREAM

1 cup (125g, 4oz)
pistachios, roughly
chopped

1 cup (250ml, 8fl oz)
coconut cream

3 egg yolks

1 cup (250ml, 8fl oz)
almond milk

2 cups (500ml, 1pt)
thickened cream

2 tbsps stevia sugar
replacement

Extra ½ cup (60g, 2oz)
pistachios, chopped, to
serve

Preheat oven to 175°C (350°F, Gas Mark 4) and grease a baking tin.

Combine all brownie ingredients except the shaved chocolate in a food processor and blend until smooth.

Spoon mixture into baking tin. Place in the oven and bake for 20 minutes.

Allow to cool for 10 minutes, then sprinkle over the shaved chocolate while it's still warm before slicing into squares.

Can be served immediately or stored in the fridge.

To make the ice cream, heat a small frying pan over medium-high heat and dry-fry the pistachios for 4 minutes or until they begin to brown. Immediately reduce the heat to medium and stir in the coconut cream. Heat until nearly simmering, then remove from the heat and let it sit for 30 minutes to cool to room temperature. Don't proceed with the next step if the cream is warm or the egg yolks will start to cook.

Place the pistachio cream mixture in a blender along with the egg yolks, almond milk, cream and stevia. Blend until everything is combined and smooth. Place in an airtight container and refrigerate for at least 2 hours.

Place in an ice-cream machine and mix for 30 minutes, or until thickened enough to freeze. Scoop out into an ice-cream container, cover and freeze for at least 2 hours.

Serve the brownies hot with a scoop of ice cream and top with chopped pistachios.

Party Food

HOW TO PARTY, LOW SUGAR STYLE

A party without soft drinks and cake? It's a party without the sugar crashes halfway through the dancing. It's all about fibre, protein and lots of imagination. Skip store-bought lolllies, milk chocolate, or packaged and frozen goods that often contain hidden sugar. Serve (a little) fruit juice and (a lot of) flavoured water for children and offer plenty of sparkling, filtered water for everyone. Beer and wine is full of sugar. Perhaps choose a signature cocktail of vodka or rum that gives enough buzz to avoid guzzling for sweetness. Add a dash of alcohol, stir in minced ginger, a dash of juice, then fill the jugs with sparkling water, seasoned with fresh mint.

'ICE THE CAKE': There are lots of options for cake toppings without sugar. Here's an idea: chop up punnets of blueberries and blackberries and let them fall all over a pile of whole-wheat pancakes. Top those with cream whipped with desiccated coconut and vanilla extract. For 'cake' number two: serve another stack, spread with cashew butter mixed with cacao powder.

DRINK AQUA FRESCA: Add water to cubed watermelon, chopped strawberries, lime juice and unsweetened apple cider. Fill with ice right before serving. Try this with super-ripe pineapple and cucumbers.

FRUIT EVERY WAY: A party is the time for splurging on stewed stone fruits like peaches and apricots, which can be dolloped with cream and cinnamon. Or peel kiwi fruit and layer the slices with mint leaves. Freeze lemons, limes and watermelon and serve still chilled on a stick for a version of icy poles. Frozen bananas are always a hit, perhaps rolled in fresh coconut — creamy, salty and tropical.

DON'T SKIP THE CHEESE: It's variety all the way with the party cheese platter. Include white cheeses like feta and goat's cheese that are lower in fat and can be marinated and seasoned with pepper, basil, olive oil, sun-dried tomatoes and different dried fruits. Include a wheel of the beloved creamy Brie for essential indulgence.

MEAT-EATER'S PARADISE: Meat is protein and fibre to be gorged on. Chicken drumsticks are a winner and can be seasoned and marinated, baked and roasted in multiple ways. Do an around-the-world in drumsticks. For an Indian twist, season with curry or tandoori spices (which can be bought as a mix or blended at home). Serve with a dipping sauce of plain yoghurt and lemon juice. Try Thai spicing with red chilli flakes, coriander and lime juice. Go Italian with a chunky tomato sauce seasoned with red capsicum, basil and chopped mushrooms.

Thai Fishcakes

CLASSIC FINGER FOOD THAT'S EASY TO MAKE AND IS A
GENERAL ALL-ROUND PARTY PLEASER

MAKES 8

500g (1lb 2oz) white
fish fillets (such as
flathead), deboned and
roughly chopped

½ cup (20g, ¾ oz) fresh
coriander leaves

¼ cup (30g, 1oz)
cornflour

2 tbsps fish sauce

½ tsp fresh lime juice

1 tsp crushed chilli
flakes

1 tsp chilli powder

1 tbsp maple syrup

1 egg, lightly beaten

3 spring onions, finely
chopped

Salt and freshly ground
black pepper

$^1/_3$ cup (80ml, 3fl oz)
peanut oil

1 medium red chilli,
seeded and finely sliced

1 cup (30g, 1oz) mixed
salad leaves

1 lime, cut into wedges

Place the fish fillets in a food processor and pulse several times
until smooth. Add the coriander, cornflour, fish sauce, lime juice,
chilli flakes, chilli powder, maple syrup and egg, and again pulse
several times and then blend until well combined.

Remove the mixture into a large bowl. Stir in the spring onions
and a good grind of salt and pepper and mix thoroughly.

Heat the peanut oil in a large frying pan over medium heat.
Divide the fish mixture into eight equal portions. Place four
portions at a time in the pan. Cook for 4 minutes on either side
until golden brown. Remove the cooked cakes and drain on
paper towels.

Serve hot with a small amount of salad leaves and chilli strips
with a wedge of lime on the side.

Tandoori Chicken Skewers

THESE MOIST AND SPICY SKEWERS ARE A FINGER-LICKING-GOOD ADDITION TO THE PARTY PLATTER

MAKES 12

⅓ cup (75g, 3oz) tandoori paste

1 tbsp lime juice

½ cup (120ml, 4fl oz) olive oil

2 cloves garlic, crushed

¼ cup (10g, ¼ oz) thyme leaves, finely chopped

Salt and freshly ground black pepper

3 chicken breasts, cut into 3cm (1in) cubes

½ green capsicum, cut into 3cm (1in) squares

½ red capsicum, cut into 3cm (1in) squares

1 red onion, quartered and halved

Soak 12 bamboo skewers in hot water for at least 30 minutes.

Whisk together the tandoori paste, lime juice, olive oil, garlic, thyme leaves and a couple of good grinds of salt and pepper in a bowl.

Thread chicken onto skewers, alternating with pieces of capsicum and onion. Place in large flat dish and spoon over tandoori mixture. Turn to ensure even coating.

Cover and refrigerate for at least 3 hours.

Remove skewers from marinade and cook on an oiled barbecue or chargrill pan, turning and occasionally basting with the marinade, for 10 minutes or until cooked through.

Spicy Chicken Breast with Hot Mango Sauce

ENJOY THE FIERY SPICE OR TONE DOWN THE CHILLI TO MAKE
THIS A DISH FOR EVERYONE

SERVES 4

3 tbsps paprika

2 tsps cumin

1 tbsp garlic, minced

1 tsp salt

¼ tsp pepper

4 chicken breasts

MANGO SAUCE

1 large mango, peeled
and flesh roughly
chopped

1 small red onion, finely
chopped

1 bird's-eye chilli, finely
chopped

2 tbsps brown vinegar

½ tsp sea salt

½ tsp fresh ginger

¼ cup (90g, 3oz) pure
maple syrup

¼ tsp cinnamon

¼ tsp ground ginger

¼ tsp ground cumin

½ tsp cayenne pepper

1 clove garlic, minced

Place paprika, cumin, garlic, salt and pepper into a plastic bag
and shake to combine.

Add chicken breasts and seal or hold the bag tight. Shake again
to coat chicken.

Transfer chicken to a bowl and cover. Leave to marinate in the
fridge for 1–3 hours, or overnight, to absorb the flavours.

Preheat oven to 215°C (420°F, Gas Mark 7).

Arrange chicken breasts on a lined baking tray. Transfer to the
oven and bake for 25 minutes.

Place the mango sauce ingredients in a blender and puree until
smooth.

Season to taste, adding more of any of the ingredients as needed.

Pour into a small saucepan and heat until nearly boiling. Remove
from heat and let cool.

Serve the chicken with the mango sauce spooned over.

Pumpkin Quiche

SERVES 6

100g (3½ oz) butter

½ cup (125ml, 4fl oz) milk

1 cup (125g, 4oz) plain flour, sifted

1 cup (250ml, 8fl oz) cream

4 eggs, lightly beaten

220g (8oz) blue cheese, crumbled

1 cup (150g, 5oz) pumpkin, chopped into small cubes

½ tsp salt

¼ tsp pepper

Preheat oven to 200°C (400°F, Gas Mark 6) and grease a 23cm (9in) quiche dish. Heat butter and milk in a medium saucepan over a low heat, stirring until butter is melted. Add flour and whisk until mixture comes together. Remove from heat and allow to cool slightly. Roll dough out on a board. Ease into prepared dish. Line the pastry with foil and fill with baking beads or rice, then place in the oven and blind bake for 10 minutes. Remove beads and foil and return to oven to bake for a further 5 minutes. Reduce oven to 180°C (350°F, Gas Mark 4). Combine cream, eggs, blue cheese, pumpkin, salt and pepper in a mixing bowl. Pour into pastry case. Place in the oven and bake for 50 minutes, until quiche is set and pastry is golden brown.

Caesar Salad

SERVES 4

3 rashers crispy bacon, cooked

2 baby cos lettuces, cut into quarters

500g (1lb) tomatoes, quartered

4 radishes, sliced

2 tbsps Parmesan cheese, shaved

DRESSING

½ cup (125ml, 4fl oz) water

¼ cup (30g, 1oz) raw cashews

¼ cup (60ml, 2fl oz) lemon juice

⅓ cup (80ml, 3fl oz) olive oil

1 tbsp Greek yoghurt

2 tbsps apple cider vinegar

1 tsp sea salt

¼ tsp freshly ground black pepper

2 cloves garlic, chopped

2 tsps maple syrup

Arrange lettuce on serving plates and top with tomatoes, radishes and bacon. To make the dressing, place all the ingredients in a blender and blend until smooth. Add more water to thin, if required. Season with any of the dressing ingredients to taste. Spoon dressing over the top of the salad and sprinkle with Parmesan.

ICEBERG LETTUCE

Super-crunchy, light and fresh in taste, iceberg lettuce has a reputation as a mediocre lettuce, which it doesn't deserve. The summery vegetable is full of fibre and half a head contains as much vitamin K as is recommended in a day for strong bones. Its leaves are sturdy and full of water, so it's like a drink of water with fibrous oomph. The sturdy, mild iceberg leaves make an excellent salad base for pungent blue cheese, or cups for minced, marinated meats. Buds of iceberg can also be stir-fried like cabbage and remain crunchy while absorbing strong flavours — try onions, soy sauce, chilli and prawns.

Cajun-Style Slow-Roasted Pork Shoulder

PERFECT FOR A BIG FAMILY BANQUET. THIS DISH TAKES JUST A LITTLE PREP AND THEN THE OVEN DOES ALL THE WORK FOR YOU

SERVES 12

1 x 2.2kg (5lb) pork shouler, boneless or bone-in

4 small onions, thickly sliced

6 cloves garlic, keep in skins

2 cups (500ml, 1pt) chicken stock

½ cup (50g, 2oz) Cajun seasoning

¼ cup (90g, 3oz) maple syrup

¼ cup (60ml, 2fl oz) olive oil

2 tbsps salt flakes

3 limes, cut into wedges

Preheat the oven to 135°C (275°F, Gas Mark 1).

Spread the onions and garlic in a large roasting tray and pour over the chicken stock.

Combine the Cajun seasoning, maple syrup, olive oil and salt flakes in a small bowl.

Pat the pork shoulder dry with kitchen paper and score with a sharp knife. Rub vigorously all over with the spice mixture.

Place the pork on top of the onions and garlic and cover with foil.

Transfer to the oven and cook for 6–8 hours, until the pork is fork tender.

Remove the pork to a cutting board and allow to cool.

Strain the cooking liquid through a fine sieve and reserve. If the pork has a bone, remove and discard it.

Shred the meat, discarding any large pieces of fat.

Serve hot with wedges of lime on the side.

Summer Salad with Green Rhubarb

THIS SIMPLE BUT STRIKING SALAD PROVIDES AN ELEGANT AND
SOPHISTICATED ACCOMPANIMENT TO YOUR MAIN MEAL

SERVES 2

1 cup (120g, 4oz) green
rhubarb, cut into 1cm
(½ in) slices

2 tbsps orange juice

1 tsp maple syrup

1 tsp fresh ginger,
minced

2 cups (60g, 2oz) mixed
salad leaves, washed,
dried and roughly
chopped

80g (3oz) Greek feta
cheese, crumbled

½ cup (80g, 3oz) raisins

¾ cup (90g, 3oz)
walnuts

DRESSING

¼ cup (60ml, 2fl oz)
orange juice

1 tbsp olive oil

1 tsp Dijon mustard

1 tsp honey

Heat a small frying pan over medium-high heat and dry-fry the
walnuts for 5 minutes or until they begin to brown. Remove
immediately from the pan and set aside.

Heat the rhubarb, orange juice, maple syrup and ginger in a
small saucepan until boiling. Reduce the heat to low and simmer
for 5 minutes, stirring gently so as not to break up the rhubarb.
The rhubarb should have softened but still retain its shape.
Remove from heat, drain the rhubarb (reserve the liquid) and let
cool for at least 1 hour.

To make the dressing, whisk together the reserved rhubarb
liquid, orange juice, oil, mustard and honey.

To assemble, place the salad leaves on a serving plate and top
with the rhubarb, raisins, walnuts and feta. Drizzle the dressing
over the top and serve.

Note: You can use red rhubarb in this salad if green is not
available or easy to find.

Jerk Chicken

SMOKY, SPICY AND A LITTLE BIT STICKY — DON'T FORGET THE NAPKINS!

MAKES 16

16 chicken drumsticks

lime wedges, to serve

¼ cup (10g, ¼ oz) fresh parsley leaves, finely chopped, to garnish

MARINADE

3 spring onions, chopped

4 cloves garlic, chopped

1 onion, chopped

3 habanero chillies, seeded

¼ cup (60ml, 2fl oz) fresh lime juice

2 tbsps soy sauce

3 tbsps olive oil

1 tbsp tomato paste

1 tbsp salt

1 tbsp brown sugar

1 tbsp fresh or dried thyme

2 tsps ground allspice

1 tsp pepper

1 tsp smoked paprika

½ tsp cinnamon

Place all the marinade ingredients in blender and process until smooth.

Place chicken and marinade in a large bowl or sealable plastic bags. Rub marinade into chicken with your hands and cover bowl or press excess air from bags, seal, then turn over several times to distribute marinade. Transfer to fridge and chill for 24 hours, turning once or twice.

Remove chicken from fridge 1 hour before cooking and place in a heatproof dish.

Preheat burners of gas grill to high. Adjust heat to moderate before placing chicken underneath. Cook for 15 minutes or until well browned on all sides. Adjust heat to low and cook chicken for 15 minutes until cooked through.

Serve with wedges of lime and parsley sprinkled over to garnish.

Mexican Rice

BOOST YOUR HUMBLE RICE SIDE DISH WITH THIS CRUNCHY
AND FRESH COMBINATION OF FLAVOURS AND TEXTURES

SERVES 6

1 cup (155g, 4oz) rice

1 x 400g (14oz) can diced tomatoes

1 x 400g (14oz) can kidney beans, rinsed and drained

2 tbsps olive oil

5 cloves garlic, finely chopped

1 fresh jalapeño chilli, seeds removed and finely chopped

1 tsp ground cumin

1 cup (170g, 6oz) fresh corn kernels

300g (10oz) green beans, ends trimmed, cut into 2cm (1in) pieces

1 tsp salt

1 tsp chilli powder

1 pomegranate, seeded

¼ cup (10g, ¼ oz) fresh coriander leaves, chopped

Combine the rice with 2 cups (500ml, 1pt) cold, salted water in a large saucepan over a medium-high heat and bring to the boil. Cover the pan and reduce the heat to low. Cook for 20 minutes, then remove from the heat and let the pan stand for a further 5 minutes.

Meanwhile, drain the can of tomatoes, retaining the juice. Combine the juice with enough water to make 1 cup (250ml, 8fl oz).

Heat the oil in a large frying pan over medium-high heat. Add the garlic and jalapeño pepper and cook for 1–2 minutes until fragrant. Don't allow the garlic to get brown. Add the cumin and fry for a further 1 minute.

Add the kidney beans, corn kernels, green beans, salt and chilli powder and cook, stirring, for 1 minute. Stir in the tomato juice and water and bring to a boil. Reduce the heat to a gentle boil and cook, stirring occasionally, for 5 minutes until most of the liquid has been absorbed.

Add the tomatoes, pomegranate, coriander, and cooked rice and cook for 1–2 minutes until the rice is warm. Serve hot.

Watermelon Salad

SERVES 8

4 large tomatoes, cut into slices

250g (9oz) yellow cherry tomatoes, halved

1 small seedless watermelon, cut into 3cm (1in) cubes

1 red onion, quartered and thinly sliced

1 tsp sea salt

1 cup (45g, 1½ oz) mint leaves, roughly chopped

2 cups (60g, 2oz) rocket leaves, washed and dried

1 cup (110g, 4oz) Greek feta cheese, crumbled

DRESSING

3 tbsps agave syrup

¼ cup (60ml, 2fl oz) balsamic vinegar

1 tbsp American mustard

Pinch of sea salt and freshly ground black pepper

1 clove garlic, crushed

¾ cup (185ml, 6fl oz) olive oil

Mix tomatoes, watermelon and onion in a mixing bowl and toss to combine. Add salt and let stand 5 to 10 minutes. In a small mixing bowl, whisk together agave, balsamic vinegar, mustard, salt, pepper and garlic. Slowly add the olive oil, while whisking, until thickened and almost creamy. Add the mint, rocket and feta to the bowl, then the dressing, and toss gently to combine.

Pork Sausage Rolls

MAKES 16

2 sheets puff pastry

550g (1¼ lb) pork mince

½ cup (75g, 3oz) apple, grated

1 onion, finely diced

1 carrot, finely grated

¼ cup (10g, ¼ oz) sage, chopped

1 egg, beaten with ½ cup (125ml, 4fl oz) milk

2 tbsps caraway seeds

Preheat oven to 180°C (350°F, Gas Mark 4). Cut each sheet of pastry in half. Mix mince with grated apple, diced onion, carrot and sage. Divide the mix into 4 even portions and lie on each pastry rectangle. Roll one edge of the pastry and tuck the sausage mix evenly under pastry. Brush egg wash on the other edge and roll the pastry on top. Slice into 4 and place on an oven tray lined with baking paper. Repeat until all the sausage mix is rolled and placed on trays. Brush each roll with egg wash, sprinkle with caraway seeds and cook for around 20–25 minutes until pastry is golden brown.

MAKE SHAPES

Carve a star out of a kiwi fruit or a loveheart into a fresh slice of honeydew melon and nobody will notice that there is no packaged candy on offer at the party. People eat with their eyes first — flavour needs imagination. A piece of rye toast can taste positively fruity in the silhouette shape of a pineapple, and a frozen strawberry on a stick is far more enticing than a bowl of high-fructose sorbet. Arrange tiny roasted florets of broccoli into the shape of a giant flowering tree and use pine nuts as blossoms. Children will eat their greens without noticing it.

WATERMELON

Crisp, juicy, fleshy watermelon: it's a winner at a party in summer and a reminder of warm seasons when tossed into a salad for a winter barbecue. Those velvety red triangles can feed a gathering craving sugar, and are also delicious when juiced — alcohol is barely missed in fresh, zesty faux cocktails.

Watermelon will satisfy the sweet tooth, as it is higher on the fructose scale than berries and a little lower in fibre. Nutritionists will recommend portion control for this reason. Yet, the good stuff it brings totally justifies the natural sugar rush: watermelon is high in lycopene, which makes the fruit red, just like tomatoes. Lycopene is excellent for cardiovascular and bone health and it has also been linked to lower rates of cancers, including prostate cancer. One chunky wedge of the fruit also packs in about one-third of the daily requirements of vitamins A and C. It's also got a nice dose of potassium, which is good for the heart and said to be great for the nerves. (Performers eat bananas and watermelon to mellow out their stage fright!)

WATERMELON A FEW WAYS

WATERMELON GRANITA: With a super-fresh, ripe watermelon, this usually sugary dessert needs no extra sugar. It all comes from the fruit. Puree watermelon with lime juice, salt and a good dose of cayenne pepper for a bit of bite. Strain and freeze the juice for up to 4 hours, breaking it up with a fork or potato masher every 20 minutes or so. This creates a salty, spicy, sugary crush. Serve in glasses with long-stemmed spoons and feel tropical.

WATERMELON, YOGHURT AND FRIED ROSEMARY SALAD: The creamy yoghurt packs in some protein to help break down more of the watermelon's sugar. Blend a spoon of raw honey into a pot of creamy yoghurt and lather it in heaps over a serving plate. Squeeze the juice from three grapefruits into a bowl, season with sea salt flakes and toss hearty cubes of watermelon through this juice. Layer the watermelon on the yoghurt. Sizzle up sprigs of rosemary in a pan of warm olive oil and sprinkle over the salad.

TOMATO AND WATERMELON GAZPACHO: It's a double dose of lycopene in a savoury dish with only natural sugar and a lot of spice. Blend tomatoes with healthy portions of garlic, onion, celery and basil, olive oil and red wine vinegar. Add a quarter of the amount of watermelon. Season with as much red hot chilli as desired. Serve chilled from the fridge with a garnish of crumbled feta cheese, which adds a creamy contrast.

Chicken Salad with Watermelon

THIS FRESH SALAD WILL BRIGHTEN UP ANY PICNIC SPREAD
AND GIVE EVERYONE A NICE ENERGY BOOST

SERVES 2–4

2 tbsps olive oil

2 tsps dried mixed herbs

1 tsp lemon zest

¼ tsp salt

Freshly ground pepper

500g (1lb) chicken breasts, skin removed

1 cup (250ml, 8fl oz) balsamic vinegar

2 cups (300g, 10oz) cubed watermelon

1 cup (110g, 4oz) Greek feta cheese, crumbled

½ cup (20g, ¾ oz) fresh parsley leaves

Whisk together the oil, dried herbs, zest, salt and pepper in a small bowl. Rub all over the chicken and let sit for at least 30 minutes in the fridge.

Heat a grill plate or barbecue grill to high heat, then grill the chicken breasts for 5 minutes on either side, or until completely cooked through. Shred the chicken into bite-sized pieces. Let cool for 15 minutes, then place in the fridge to cool for at least 1 hour.

Bring the balsamic vinegar to a boil in a small saucepan. Reduce the heat to low and simmer, covered, for 20 minutes until reduced by at least one-quarter and thickened to a syrup.

Place the watermelon, feta, chicken and parsley in a salad bowl and toss to combine.

Serve drizzled with balsamic vinegar.

Seared Scallops with Sesame Butter

DON'T BE SCARED OF SCALLOPS! THIS EASY RECIPE PROVIDES A SURE-FIRE WAY TO MAKE THEM A GREAT SUCCESS AT YOUR DINNER PARTY

SERVES 4

¼ cup (40g, 1½ oz) white sesame seeds

2 tsps black sesame seeds

2 bunches asparagus, woody ends trimmed

1 cup (170g, 6oz) fresh peas, shelled

16 large scallops

80g (3oz) unsalted butter

2 tsps paprika

1 tsp sea salt

½ tsp ground coloured peppercorns

1 lemon, cut into wedges, to garnish

Heat a small frying pan over medium-high heat and dry-fry the sesame seeds for 1 minute. Remove immediately from the pan and set aside.

Fill a large saucepan with lightly salted water and boil the asparagus and peas for 2 minutes. Immediately drain and set aside.

Pat scallops dry with paper towel.

Heat a large heavy-based frying pan over medium-high heat. Melt the butter with the sesame seeds, paprika, salt and ground peppercorns. Fry the scallops in batches for 4 minutes, turning halfway through, until cooked through but slightly translucent in the centre. Ensure each side is coated with sesame seeds.

To serve, place the scallops on a bed of asparagus and peas. Sprinkle with leftover sesame seeds from the frying pan.

Sprinkle over some more ground peppercorns and serve with a wedge of lemon on the side.

Teriyaki Salmon with Black Soba Noodles and Asparagus

COLOURFUL, DRAMATIC AND SOPHISTICATED, THIS MIGHT BECOME YOUR DINNER PARTY GO-TO DISH

SERVES 4

1 tbsp fresh ginger, minced

1 bird's-eye chilli, seeds removed, minced

1 tsp freshly ground black pepper

2 tbsps tamari

2 tbsps sake

1 tbsp rice wine vinegar

1 tbsp maple syrup

4 x 150g (5oz) salmon fillets, skin on, bones removed

270g (9oz) pkt black soba noodles

3 tsps sesame oil

2 bunches asparagus, woody ends trimmed

1 bunch garlic chives with flowers intact, cut in half

¼ cup (10g, ¼ oz) chervil leaves

Combine the ginger, chilli, pepper, tamari, sake, rice wine vinegar and maple syrup in a small saucepan over low heat. Stir for 3 minutes, then remove from heat and set aside to cool for at least 15 minutes.

Place the salmon in a shallow container and pour the tamari mixture over the top. Turn the fillets a couple of times to coat then cover the container with plastic wrap.

Place in the fridge for at least 30 minutes.

Cook the noodles according to packet instructions. Drain and stir through 1 teaspoon sesame oil to prevent them from sticking together, and set aside.

Bring a pot of salted water to the boil and cook the asparagus for 2 minutes. Drain and divide among serving plates.

Drain the salmon, reserving the leftover marinade liquid.

Heat 1 teaspoon sesame oil in a large frying pan over medium-high heat. Cook the salmon for 2 minutes, skin side up. Flip over and cook for a further 3 minutes until cooked through. Remove from the pan and transfer to a plate and cover with foil.

Heat the rest of the sesame oil in the frying pan. Add the chive flowers and stems to the pan and fry for 2 minutes, stirring constantly and set aside.

Add the reserved marinade and bring to the boil for 1 minute. Add the noodles and stir to heat them through.

Divide the noodles over the asparagus on the serving plates, top with the chives, a piece of salmon and a couple of chervil leaves to garnish.

Fried Whitebait with Mayo

SERVES 6

Canola oil, for deep-frying

2 eggs and 2 tbsps water, lightly beaten

1 cup (125g, 4oz) tapioca flour

1 tbsp smoked paprika

2 tbsps sea salt

1kg (2lb) whitebait, rinsed and patted dry

1 lemon, cut into wedges

CHILLI LIME MAYO

1 cup (250ml, 8fl oz) mayonnaise (see recipe page 72)

1 tsp sweet chilli sauce

1 tsp lime zest

1 tsp lime juice

Heat oil in a wok or deep-fryer to 180°C (350°F). Whisk together the mayo ingredients in a small bowl. Set aside. Place egg and water mix in a shallow bowl. Mix the tapioca flour with paprika and salt and place in a medium bowl. Dip whitebait in the egg mixture, shake off excess and then toss in the tapioca flour to coat. Fry the fish in the hot oil for 2 minutes or until golden, and remove with a slotted spoon. Drain on paper towels, sprinkle with salt and serve immediately, garnished with parsley, with lemon wedges and mayonnaise.

Mini Rosti with Salmon

MAKES 16

6 medium potatoes, peeled and grated (use a waxy variety such as desiree or coliban)

1 tsp sea salt

½ tsp freshly ground black pepper

1 cup (250ml, 8fl oz) vegetable oil for frying

1 cup (250ml, 8fl oz) chilli lime mayo (see recipe on this page)

½ cup (20g, ¾ oz) dill, roughly chopped

200g (7oz) smoked salmon slices, cut into 16 bite-sized pieces

Place the grated potato in a colander and squeeze it to remove as much excess liquid as you can. Pat dry with paper towels. Mix the potato together with the salt and pepper. Heat the oil in a large frying pan to 5mm (¼ in) deep over medium-high heat. Place dessertspoons of the rosti mixture into the pan and flatten with a spatula. You should get at least 16 rosti. Fry for 3 minutes either side until crispy and golden on the outside. Drain on paper towels and repeat until all the mixture has been used. Serve with a dollop of chilli lime mayo on top, plus a piece of salmon, and a small amount of dill to garnish.

PICKLED BEETROOT

Vinegary, crunchy and naturally sweet, pickled beetroot is like savoury candy, bursting with iron and antioxidants and nitrates that boost oxygen to the brain and help blood circulation. Pickle it at home with different seasonings — try fragrant rosemary and lemon, or Indian spices such as cumin, coriander and mustard seeds that will transform a slice of cheese into a spicy, fruity bite. Scoop pickled beetroot onto boiled or deviled eggs and serve them as finger food. Stir it into a bowl of yoghurt, or add a burst of juicy purple to sour cream, mayonnaise or yoghurt to dollop onto fritters made from zucchini.

BRIE AND CAMEMBERT

When leaving sugar behind, it's important to have rewards, as it's not easy. The cheese plate is a good way to go. And, as research continues to show, fat is an essential naughty — it keeps the belly full, and it's no small gift how deeply satisfying it is to eat.

It doesn't get much more indulgent than the two classics: Brie and Camembert. Both are rich, full fat cheeses made from cow's milk and aged in a chewy, white rind. Are they the same thing? Nope.

Brie is creamier with a higher fat content than Camembert. When sliced open and into triangles, the insides of Brie might ooze onto the cheese platter, perfect for scooping up with a cheese knife (or a sneaky finger) and lathering over a rice cracker. Brie comes from Ile-de-France, a region in north-central France.

Camembert comes from a little further north, from the region of Normandy where there is a town called Camembert. This region continues to export and inspire gorgeous, pungent wheels of rich, almost bouncy Camembert throughout the world. Camembert is more savoury and robust than Brie — the ooze is less likely, and while Brie smells like butter, Camembert might have a very light mushroomy and possibly garlicky odour. Camembert will be a little more yellow to Brie's clean white colour. Camembert is made for baking and serving with a fruit. It is also the better choice for slicing onto baguettes with leaves of peppery rocket and prosciutto.

Brie is made for spreading its goo over toasted rye bread. Or, for a major treat, Brie is sometimes fried — the rind is dusted in flour and egg and becomes crunchy and crumbly around the soft cheese. A lemony flavour may be released, which is a perfect tang for the sweet, buttery warm cheese.

TWO DECADENT DISHES

BAKED BRIE WITH GARLIC AND THYME: Stuff a wheel of cheese with a garlic clove and sprigs of thyme to infuse an earthy, peppery fragrance. Bake at 180°C (350°F) for around 15 minutes, until there's a light crunch on the rind and a dip in the middle where the cheese is beginning to melt. Serve with plenty of knives to scoop up the cream.

PROSCIUTTO-WRAPPED BAKED CAMEMBERT: This is as simple to cook as it sounds, yet anything but simple to taste. Layer a few sage leaves on a wheel of Camembert — sage is strong and lemony and blends with the salt and fat of the cheese and meat. Wrap very thin slices of prosciutto around the whole wheel. Bake for 15 minutes — the prosciutto will crisp and the cheese will soften. Divine.

Baked Camembert Wheel

SIMPLE BUT UTTERLY DECADENT AND DELICIOUS, THIS IS A TREAT YOUR DINERS ARE SURE TO APPRECIATE

SERVES 4

1 whole Camembert wheel, in a wooden box

2 tsps honey

¼ cup (60ml, 2fl oz) olive oil

2 sprigs of rosemary

2 sprigs lavender flowers

1 clove garlic, crushed

Sea salt flakes and black pepper, to taste

1 small French stick of sourdough, cut into 1cm (½ in) thick slices

Preheat oven to 180°C (350°F, Gas Mark 5).

Remove the Camembert from the wrapper and place back in the wooden box.

Using a sharp knife, cut a 3mm (1/8 in) deep crosshatch into the top of the Camembert wheel. Place the box in a small baking dish.

Drizzle the honey and 2 teaspoons of olive oil over the top of the cheese. Sprinkle over a couple of rosemary leaves and lavender flowers.

Bake in the over for 20 minutes, or until the Camembert is softened. Remove from the box and place on a preheated serving dish.

While the Camembert is baking, heat a large frying pan over medium-high heat.

Mix the garlic with the rest of the oil and brush over the sourdough bread slices. Fry the slices in the pan in batches for 1 minute either side until browned.

Serve the toasted sourdough with the melted Camembert and garnish with rosemary and lavender.

Coconut and Honey Layered Cake with Cashew Cream

THIS LUXURIOUS CAKE TAKES A LITTLE TIME AND FOCUS AND DELIVERS A LIGHT, CREAMY, SWEET, INDULGENT TREAT IN RETURN

SERVES 12

4 tbsps honey

½ cup (110g, 4oz) stevia sugar replacement

¼ cup (90g, 3oz) maple syrup

2 tbsp unsalted butter

3 large eggs, lightly beaten

3 cups (375g, 12oz) gluten-free plain flour

1 tsp bicarbonate of soda

1 tsp cinnamon

1 tsp orange zest

CASHEW CREAM

3 cups (375g, 13oz) cashews, soaked for 2 hours

2 tbsps lemon juice

3 tbsps coconut oil

½ cup (180g, 6oz) maple syrup

Water, as needed

TOPPING

1 cup (120g, 4oz) almond meal

1 cup (90g, 3oz) desiccated coconut

Preheat oven to 180°C (350°F, Gas Mark 5). Line a large flat baking tray with baking paper.

To make the cashew cream, soak the cashews in a bowl of water overnight. Strain the cashews and place in a blender with the lemon juice, coconut oil, maple syrup, and as much water as needed to puree until smooth. Place in the fridge to firm up.

Heat the honey, stevia, maple syrup and butter in a medium saucepan over medium heat for 5 minutes until the sugar is dissolved. Remove the pot from the heat and let it cool for 10 minutes. Then add the eggs slowly in a steady stream, stirring vigorously the whole time. Mix together the flour, bicarb, cinnamon and zest in a large mixing bowl. Stir the honey mixture into the dry ingredients until everything is thoroughly combined. It should reach an almost clay-like consistency.

Working quickly to keep the dough warm, split it into 5 equal pieces. Roll out each piece on a lightly floured surface into a circle about 4mm (1/8 in) thick. Use a 23cm (9in) diameter plate or cake tin to cut out a perfect circle from each piece of dough.

Bake 2 rounds at a time, each for 5 minutes, until golden. Carefully transfer to wire rack and repeat until the rest of the rounds have been cooked. Set aside to cool.

Spread out the almond meal and coconut on the baking tray and bake for 15 minutes or until they are toasted and golden. Remove from the oven and set aside.

Assemble the cake by spreading each round with about one-third of a cup of the cashew cream. Stack layers on top of each other, then frost the entire outside of the cake with the remaining cashew cream. Sprinkle toasted almond meal and coconut over the cake and press into the cream.

Cover the cake with plastic wrap and place in the fridge overnight before eating so the cream soaks into the cake.

Raw Banana Nut Cheesecake

IF YOU'VE NEVER TASTED OR SERVED A RAW CHEESECAKE,
NOW'S YOUR CHANCE. THIS RECIPE IS A CINCH

SERVES 12

BASE

½ cup (60g, 2oz) raw almonds

½ cup (60g, 2oz) raw pistachio nuts

¾ cup (60g, 2oz) desiccated coconut

⅓ cup (55g, 2oz) buckwheat groats

¾ cup (130g, 4oz) medjool dates, pitted

1 tbsp raw cacao powder

3 tsps rice malt syrup

Pinch of sea salt

CHEESECAKE

½ cup (120g, 4oz) cacao butter, grated

2½ cups (310g, 10oz) raw cashews, soaked in water overnight

½ tsp vanilla extract

½ cup (180g, 6oz) rice malt syrup

½ cup (125ml, 4fl oz) coconut cream

TO SERVE

3 ripe bananas, sliced

Mint leaves, to garnish

Place the almonds, pistachios, coconut and buckwheat into a high-speed blender or food processor. Pulse several times until fine crumbs form. Add the dates, cacao, rice malt syrup and salt and process until the mixture comes together in a dough-like consistency.

Press the mixture into the bottom of a 28 x 18cm (11 x 7in) deep-sided baking tray. Place in the fridge to chill while you make the topping.

Place the cacao butter for the cheesecake layer in a heatproof bowl over a pan of gently simmering water until melted.

Using a high-speed blender, blend the cashews, vanilla, rice malt syrup and coconut cream for 2 minutes, or until very smooth. Add melted cacao butter and blend for a further 1 minute until very creamy.

Remove base from the fridge and pour the cream mixture on top.

Return to the freezer for 3 hours or until completely set.

Decorate with slices of banana. Cut into 12 blocks and serve garnished with fresh mint leaves.

Almond Milk Chocolate Pudding

THIS CREAMY CHOCOLATE DESSERT IS A FANTASTIC OPTION FOR DAIRY-FREE DINERS

SERVES 2–4

2 cups (500ml, 1pt) almond milk

½ cup (180g, 6oz) rice malt syrup

4 tbsps cornflour

2 tbsps chilled water

Pinch of sea salt

1 tsp vanilla extract

1 tsp cinnamon

1 tbsp raw cacao powder

CREAM

1 x 400g (14oz) can organic coconut milk, chilled

2 tsps maple syrup

1 tbsp raw cacao powder

4 fresh strawberries

Heat the almond milk in a small saucepan over medium-high heat and stir in the rice malt syrup.

Mix the cornflour together in a small glass with the cold water.

Add the cornflour gradually to the milk, stirring vigorously to prevent lumps forming. Add the salt, vanilla, cinnamon and cacao powder and stir until it begins to boil. Remove from the heat and stir for 1 minute, then let it sit until it reaches room temperature. Then chill in the fridge for at least 2 hours before going to the next step.

When you open the can of coconut milk, scoop out the thickened cream part that sits at the top. This is the cream you will use for whipping. Keep the rest of the milk for another use.

Whip the cream together with the maple syrup and cacao until light and fluffy.

Fold the coconut cream into the chilled almond mixture with a slotted spoon until just combined.

Spoon the pudding mix into your dessert glasses or bowls and chill in the fridge for at least 2 hours before serving.

Serve with a fresh strawberry to garnish.

Index

erythritol 209

fish, *see also* **tuna**
baked blue-eye with anchovy crust 122
baked salmon with vegetables 114
fried whitebait with mayo 288
mini rosti with salmon 288
teriyaki salmon with black soba noodles
and asparagus 286
Thai fishcakes 258

flaxseeds 17

flours 185

freekeh 79
smoked chicken and sprout salad 80

honey 209
coconut and honey layered cake with
cashew cream 294

horseradish 119

iceberg lettuce 265

kale 180
kale chips 181
superfoods salad 76

lamb
moussaka 116

leek
chicken and leek tartlets 90

lemon
lemon cake with cashew frosting 216
poppyseed and lemon muffins 190
poppyseed lemon pancakes 190

lime 135
key lime cheesecake 210
lime and pepper grilled chicken
breast 136
summer fruits and goat's cheese salad
with lime vinaigrette 98

mango
melon and mango refresher 18
spicy chicken breast with hot mango
sauce 262

maple syrup 209

matcha 25
matcha chia pudding 24
matcha green tea brownie 24
matcha green tea madeleines 192
matcha smoothie bowl 18

miso
chicken and noodle miso soup with
egg 92

mushroom
brown rice risotto 118
hot Japanese ramen 128
portobello mushroom burger 86

Natvia 209

noodles
chicken and noodle miso soup with
egg 92
hot Japanese ramen 128
soba noodle stir-fry with beef and
vegetables 130
teriyaki salmon with black soba noodles
and asparagus 286

oats
fruit and oat vegan cookies 200
oatmeal cookies 194
overnight oat and chia pudding 30

orange
orange and poppyseed slice 188
orange poppyseed dressing 72

passionfruit
passionfruit chia pudding 162

pastry
cabbage and sausage strudel 68
mille feuille with raspberries and
cream 236
poppyseed pie 186
pork sausage rolls 276
summer tart 164
white bean and carrot hummus tartlets
with coriander pesto 56

peach
peach and three cheese pizza 100

peanut butter
chocolate Irish cream dessert 246

pear 215
baked pears with fruit and nut 214
pear pie with cinnamon 214

pistachios
black bean brownie with pistachio ice
cream 248
raw banana nut cheesecake 296

polenta
breakfast polenta with Greek yoghurt
and raspberries 34
cheesy polenta with pesto and roasted
spicy chickpeas 44

pomegranate
black rice and pomegranate salad
bowl 42

poppyseeds 191
orange and poppyseed slice 188
poppyseed and lemon muffins 190
poppyseed lemon pancakes 190
poppyseed pie 186

pork
Cajun-style slow-roasted pork
shoulder 266
pork larb lettuce wraps 138
pork meatballs with garlic yoghurt
dip 120
pork sausage rolls 276

potato
mini rosti with salmon 288

pumpkin
almond and pumpkin breakfast
porridge 36
grilled pumpkin salad 90
pumpkin quiche 264
pumpkin syrup pie 166
quinoa and pumpkin gratin 66
quinoa stuffed pumpkin 82
spicy pumpkin and walnut slice 168

quinoa
dark chocolate quinoa breakfast
bowl 22
quinoa and pumpkin gratin 66
quinoa basil salad with poached egg 52
quinoa stuffed pumpkin 82
superfoods salad 76
zucchini and quinoa muffins 172

raspberries
breakfast polenta with Greek yoghurt
and raspberries 34
mille feuille with raspberries and
cream 236
semolina raspberry cake 220
Victoria layer cake with cream and
raspberries 232

rhubarb
summer salad with green rhubarb 268

rice
black rice and pomegranate salad
bowl 42
brown rice risotto 118
Mexican rice 274
risotto with pork sausage and
vegetables 152

rice malt syrup 209

sausage
cabbage and sausage strudel 68
egg, chorizo and cheese tarts 176
risotto with pork sausage and
vegetables 152

scallops
seared scallops with sesame butter 284

semolina
semolina raspberry cake 220

spinach 173
bean and barley porridge with
spinach 148
green pancakes 172
green scrambled eggs 48
mozzarella and spinach tart 174
spinach and tuna quiche 88
spinach and ricotta rolls 102

stevia 209

strawberries
ricotta pancakes and strawberries 104
strawberry cream parfait 234

sweet potato
veggie chips 181

tarragon 143
chicken with tarragon sauce 142

tofu
vegan chocolate cake with cashew
cream 242

tuna
spinach and tuna quiche 88

turkey
turkey meatballs with barley 150

vanilla 239
vanilla custard 244

walnuts
baked pears with fruit and nut 214
berry tart with a walnut crust 226
grain-free muesli 32
spicy pumpkin and walnut slice 168

watermelon 281
chicken salad with watermelon 282
watermelon salad 276

yoghurt
breakfast polenta with Greek yoghurt
and raspberries 34
pork meatballs with garlic yoghurt
dip 120

zucchini
zucchini and quinoa muffins 172

First Published in 2017 by Herron Book Distributors Pty Ltd
14 Manton St
Morningside
QLD 4170
www.herronbooks.com

Custom book production by Captain Honey Pty Ltd
PO Box 155
Byron Bay
NSW 2481
www.captainhoney.com.au

Cataloguing-in-Publication. A catalogue record for this book is available from the National Library of Australia

ISBN 978-0-947163-65-5

Printed and bound in China by Shenzhen Jinhao Color Printing Co., Ltd

5 4 3 2 1   17 18 19 20 21

NOTES FOR THE READER

All reasonable efforts have been made to ensure the accuracy of the content in this book. Information in this book is not intended as a substitute for medical advice. The author and publisher cannot and do not accept any legal duty of care or responsibility in relation to the content in this book, and disclaim any liabilities relating to its use.

PHOTO CREDITS

Front cover: Natasha Breen
Back cover: Nataliya Arzamasova
5PH p 143. alicja neumiler p 265. Africa Studio p 280. Antonina Vlasova p 170. Anna_Pustynnikova p 24, 173, 290, 102, 249. Alena Ozerova p 14. Armushik p 142. Aimee M Lee p 227. Armushik p 75, 145. aliasemma p 101. Avdeyukphoto p 50. Anna Hoychuk p 179, 182. Ahmet Yasti p 94. agrofruti p 202. Bartosz Luczak p 139. Brent Hofacker p 160. casanisa p 4. Cristian Sabau p 49. CaseyMartin p 190. Cesarz p 102. Charlotte Lake p 288. CBCK p 288. ch_ch p 156. Djero Adlibeshe p 204. Dominik Demcak p 1, 13, 61, 109, 157, 205, 253. Diana Taliun p 191. Daxiao Productions p 2, 177, 184, 256. Elena Shashkina p 244. Elena Veselova p 119, 278, 264. Evgeny Karandaev p 230. Elza Brop p 35, 37. Elizaveta Galitckaia p 277. Elena Veselova p 269. Ekaterina Kondratova p224. Elena Veselova p 163. FoodPhotoAtelier p 187. Foxys Forest Manufacture p58, 96. George Dolgikh p 125. Gaus Nataliya p 181. Gayvoronskaya_Yana p 12. hlphoto p 89, 117, 175. Halfpoint p 110, 123. Ivanna Grigorova p 72. inthason99 p 25. iuliia_n p 47, 90, 125, 193, 221. iian_angle p 106. Igor Normann p 228. Jan Wischnewski p 287. jose115 p 259. Kateryna Abramova p 225. Karpenkov Denis p 81. Krunja p 129. Kade Sudkamon p 29. Katarzyna Hurova p 91. Khakimullin Aleksandr p 60. Lilly Trott p 33. Igabriela p 118. Lisovskaya Natalia p 131, 293. Losangela p 10. Liliya Kandrashevich p 190. Lapina Maria p 172. little lulu p 206. Maren Winter p 112. MaraZe p 73, 244. mama_mia p 241. Magdalena Paluchowska p 238. matka_Wariatka p 19. Marian Weyo p 126. MariaKovaleva p 169. Nataliya Arzamasova p 6, 23, 31, 43, 45, 53, 57, 201, 235, 149, 158, 195, 199, 211, 243, 247, 297, 299. NSphotostudio p 250. Natasha Breen p 237, 300. neil langan p 78. NoirChocolate p 65, 69, 189, 214. Olexiy Bayev p 70, 108, 118, 267, 254. oneinchpunch p 252. Ollinka p 146. Phototasty p 93, 137, 263, 270, 275, 276. Pushish Images p 134. Petar Bogdanov p 215. pearl7 p 121, 217, 233, 295. Pinkyone p 181. Paulo Vilela p 26. Quanthem p28. rodrigobark p 208. Rawpixel.com p 154. SEAGULL_L p 167, 264. saschanti17 p 180. Syda Productions p 40. Showroom Photos Stock p 196. Saharosa40 p 213. Svetlana Bunchukova p 24. sarsmis p 99, 224, 276. stockcreations p 273. Timolina p 115. teleginatania p 67, 83, 151, 165, 223. Tatiana Vorona p 289. Tatyana Malova p 132. TravnikovStudio p 218. Tirik p 172. vanillaechoes p 72. VICUSCHKA p 261. Viktory Panchenko p 285. Viktoria Hodos p 105. vanillaechoes p 90. wason yuyatmak p 55. Wiktory p 283. YuliiaKas p 12. Yulia Grigoryeva p 84. Yulia Furman p 245. Zhuravleva p 153. zarzamora p 16, 18, 21, 29, 38, 87, 103. Zoe Jane McClean p 77, 141. Images used under license from Shutterstock.com